THE STATE OF GIVING RESEARCH IN EU

The State of Giving Research in Europe

Household Donations to Charitable Organizations in Twelve European Countries

EDITED BY
PAMALA WIEPKING

PALLAS PUBLICATIONS

Cover design: René Staelenberg, Amsterdam
Layout: Sophie de Wijs

ISBN 978 90 8555 009 9
e- ISBN 978 90 4851 089 4
NUR 756

© European Research Network on Philanthropy (ERNOP) /
Amsterdam University Press, Amsterdam 2009

Contents

Introduction
Theo Schuyt[1]

All 27 European states belonging to the European Community are governed through democratic systems. They are all welfare states, which means that a certain level of social solidarity is guaranteed by governments in the context of a free market economy and a plural polity.

These societal infrastructures—including the underlying philosophical, cultural and political theories and principles—were in an integrated way, first propagated during the French Revolution. Its famous parole: Liberté, Egalité, Fraternité presents the interrelatedness of market, government and philanthropy. At an even earlier date in Europe, philanthropy had already been legally codified through the Charity Law of Queen Elizabeth in 1601.

Philanthropy is rooted in the Christian and Jewish European traditions as well as the Islamic religion of today. Till the 1990s, the only country in the world in which the macro-economic volume of philanthropy had been systematically described was the United States. In this country, the American Association of Fund Raising Counsel (AAFRC) at the University of Indianapolis (Center for the Study of Philanthropy) has been publishing "Giving USA", a report on philanthropy in de United States, on a yearly basis since 1955. The Netherlands is the only Western European country in which similar research has been conducted. In 1993, the VU University Amsterdam started its two-yearly publication of "Giving the Netherlands". Now the time has come to bring philanthropy to the front of the European stage again.

The Giving Europe research project aims to present the financial parameters of the philanthropic sector in EC member states. As a result, structured and comparable micro- and macro-economic estimations of the content of the philanthropic contributions will be available per nation, and within a time-span of several years, for the EC as a whole.

In doing so, the project tries to enhance the insights into the potentials of the rising "civil society". Moreover, the project will stimulate and support the philanthropic sector in its efforts to raise professional standards and quality. A rich database will become available for fundraisers and grantmakers as well as grantseekers. For policymakers, at the national and EC levels the availability of micro- and macro-economic data and trends

---

[1] Theo Schuyt, Department of Philanthropic Studies, VU University Amsterdam, Amsterdam, the Netherlands, TNM.Schuyt@fsw.vu.nl, +31 20 5986781

concerning philanthropy will help to develop partnerships between governments and the emerging philanthropic sector. In making databases available, the project will also attract the attention of academia. Research data and longitudinal data form a solid foundation for academic projects.

To start off this research, the first step was the creation of a network of European scholars in this field. For this reason the Center for the Study of Philanthropy of the VU University Amsterdam launched the European Research Network on Philanthropy, called ERNOP. This network celebrated its first meeting in Amsterdam, January 2008. During this meeting, the academicians decided to gather data already available in their respective countries, and to trace sources of information.

This first publication is the result of their endeavours. It is a preliminary product and limited to data of household giving. Although it is a first attempt, the scholars involved strongly believe in their mission to gain attention, through this research, for the potential of philanthropy to support EC welfare states and the well-being of Europe in general.

Welfare states in Western Europe are in transition. Demographic changes, growing wealth, cultural and political developments at both national and European levels are triggering fundamental shifts in economic, social and political institutions. Western Europe has initiated the ongoing process of restructuring: integrating new East European countries on the one hand, while Western European countries cope with the ethnic diversity challenges on the other. As a result, the transition compels governments, businesses and civic efforts to continuously innovate to ensure that Western Europe remains a prosperous and democratic community to live in. Only philanthropy—voluntary action for the public good (Payton, 1988) —will be able to deliver the considerable impetus required to achieve these goals.

The pillars of future prosperity will be sustainable economic growth, political democracy, and a basic level of social services. Along with the economic and political changes, most Western European countries are transforming into so-called "civil societies". Social institutions and the "public good" in general will financially rely on three sources of contributions:
a. government funding
b. fees and charges
c. philanthropy (Salamon, et al. 2004).

This ERNOP initiative attempts to make the philanthropic efforts visible. This report contains the results of twelve countries. All chapters are arranged in the same format. First, an introduction is given to the state of giving research: what datasources are available? What kind of information do they provide? Secondly, the positive and negative aspects of these data sources are evaluated. And finally, a summary of available results and a conclusion on philanthropy is given.

This first ERNOP publication will end with conclusions on the state of giving research in Europe.

References

Payton, R.L. (1988). *Philanthropy: Voluntary Action for the Public Good.* New York, Macmillian.

Salamon, L.W., Sokolowski, S.W., et al. (2004). *Global Civil Society. Dimensions of the Nonprofit Sector.* Bloomfield, Kumarian Press.

2. The State of Giving Research in Europe

2.1 Austria
Florian Bittner[2] and Michaela Neumayr[3]

There is no central institution that investigates charitable giving in Austria. Some sources provide data on private donations:

ÖIS - Spendenbericht
The *Österreichisches Institut für Spendenwesen ÖIS (Austrian Institute of Fundraising)* records Austrian charities that call for donations publicly and regularly. As per September 2008, the ÖIS counts more than 1,100 charities.

In cooperation with other institutions (polling institute market research; polling institute Public Opinion; Institute of Social Policy, Vienna University of Economics and Business; Institute for Interdisciplinary Research on Nonprofit Organisations), the ÖIS conducts representative population surveys on charitable giving on a regular basis. These surveys were conducted in 1996, 2000, 2004, and 2008 and based on face-to-face interviews, covering about 1,000 individuals.

Since 2006, the ÖIS has published an annual report (*"ÖIS-Spendenbericht"*), which provides information on developments and perspectives on private giving in Austria.

Commercial poll data from market research: Spendenmonitor
The Austrian polling institute *market research* annually investigates private household giving. The poll covers questions on personal amounts of donations, sympathy for organisations, as well as common questions like motives and objectives. As a commercial product, the poll's results are available for a fee.

Revenues of Nonprofit Organisations from Donations
In 2006, Statistics Austria and the Institute for Social Policy (Vienna University of Economics and Business) conducted a representative survey on Nonprofit Organisations in Austria, revealing that about 8,5% of the total

---

[2] Florian Bittner, Geschäftsführung ÖFSE, Austrian Research Foundation for International Development, Vienna, Austria, office@spenden, + 43 13174010 – 105
[3] Michaela Neumayr, Research Institute for Nonprofit Organisations, Vienna University of Economics and Business, Vienna, Austria, michaela.neumayr@wu.ac.at, +43/1/31336/5111

revenues of NPOs originate from private or corporate donations (Schneider & Haider 2009).

Strengths and weaknesses of Austrian data
ÖIS surveys on private donations by individuals
Strengths:

- Surveys dating back to 1996, conducted using the same method, available
- Most of the questions comparable with those from previous years
- Wide range of background characteristics

Weaknesses:

- Most of the questions are not comparable with international survey data

However, there is some hope that the situation on data on charitable giving will improve in the near future, as in 2009 the tax law has changed and charitable giving is tax-deductible now. Thus, an additional source of data, tax records, will be available. In addition, the government plans to evaluate the effects of this change in tax law. Such an evaluation would supply more detailed information on charitable giving in Austria.

Descriptive Statistics
Referring to the Spendenstudie 2008 (Neumayr & Schober 2009), the estimated total income on donations was about 295 million euros in 2008. The average amount donated per donor was about 65,3 euros per year, which amounts to 42,0 euros per adult. About 66% of the Austrian population donates, with 'children', 'national disaster relief' and 'animals' being the most popular areas people donate for. Further information on the amount donated using different methods and on motives to donate or not to donate can be found in the Spendenstudie 2008.

References
Neumayr, M., Schober, C. (2009). *Spendenstudie 2008, Zwischenbericht,* Vienna: Forschungsinstitut für Nonprofit Organisationen, Vienna University of Economics and Business

Schneider, U., Haider, A. (2009). *Nonprofit Organisationen in Österreich 2006, Forschungsbericht,* Vienna: Institut für Sozialpolitik, Vienna University of Economics and Business

2.2 Belgium
Lesley Hustinx[4] and Caroline Gijselinckx[5]

Data sources for household donations in Belgium
There is no overall statistical source in Belgium that provides general data on charitable giving, and no systematic longitudinal data collection on charitable giving by individuals or households has been set up thus far. As a rule, scientific research is organized and funded at the regional level, resulting in relatively distinct research circuits in Flanders and Wallonia.

At the federal level, information on charitable giving can be derived from tax records on charitable deductions from the DG Statistics and Economic Information (formerly known as the National Statistical Office). In 2002, the Federal Department of Finance commissioned a study that provided information regarding the scope and functional classification of tax-deducted donations (Contactgroep Giften, 2002). An important observation was that in 1999, the amount of charitable deductions had increased by a factor of 30 compared to 1965 (corrected for inflation). In 1999, in total, Belgian households deducted about 97.9 million euros from taxes. In the same year, corporations residing in Belgium deducted some 17,3 million euros from taxes. More recent information is not available, since this was a one-off study. A parliamentary question was asked concerning whether it would be possible to replicate this study, the answer being that it would be far too costly to organize it on a regular basis, let alone an annual one. Moreover, the administration has access to limited information. There is no systematized information on legacies, donations in kind, or non-deductible gifts.

In Flanders, data on charitable giving by individuals was collected in two representative population surveys, conducted in 1991 (Van Ootegem, 1993) and in 1999 (Damen et al., 2000; Mortelmans, Damen, & Sinardet, 2005). More recent survey data are not available. In the annual population survey by the Flemish Government, there was a limited question on 'checkbook activism' in the years 2000, 2002, and 2003. To the best of our knowledge, there are no publications based on this data.

The most recent data on charitable giving by individuals were collected by researchers at the Higher Institute of Labour Studies in the context of a study on the public support of NGOs in Flanders (Pollet & Huybrechts, 2007), which was a follow-up to a similar study conducted in

[4] Lesley Hustinx, postdoctoral fellow Research Foundation - Flanders, Centre for Sociological Research (CeSO), K.U.Leuven, Leuven, Belgium, lesley.hustinx@soc.kuleuven.be, +32 16 323050
[5] Caroline Gijselinckx, Higher Institute of Labour Studies, HIVA-K.U.Leuven, Leuven, Belgium, caroline.gijselinckx@hiva.kuleuven.be, +32 16 323328

2003 and 2004 (Pollet & Develtere, 2003, 2004). The focus, however, was limited to charitable donations for third world issues.

Table 2.2.1 Strengths and weaknesses of the Belgium data sources

Strengths	Weaknesses
Federal tax records	
• Longitudinal data	• Small range of background characteristics
• Population results	• Tax deductions only apply to gifts of a minimum of EUR 30 per organization
	• A limited list of organizations (14 categories) is entitled to give tax reductions (Federale Overheidsdienst Financiën).
	• Individuals need to have a taxable income
Population surveys in Flanders	
• Representative	• One-off surveys
• Relatively comprehensive profile of the Flemish giver (socio-economic background, strategies for giving, motives for giving)	• 'Method+Area' module not used
Survey on the Public Support for NGOs in Flanders	
• Longitudinal	• Charitable giving limited to development cooperation
• Not only giving in terms of money, but also consumer behaviour and other forms of action and direct support	• Non-random sample, over-representation of those with pro-social behaviour

Descriptive statistics
In 1990, 16% of the Flemish population did not donate to charitable organizations. Of those who donated, only 16% deducted their charitable gift from their income in relation to tax breaks. The average deducted gift had a value of BEF 5051 or about 125 euros; the average non-deducted gift had a value of BEF 801 or about 20 euros. Of all private gifts, 53.8% was donated to development cooperation (Van Ootegem, 1993). In the 1999 survey conducted by the research team of Antwerp University, about 75% of

respondents reported giving to charitable causes, so the prevalence of giving in Flanders seemed to have declined in comparison to the 1990 data. The average amount of giving was estimated to be 68 euros (Mortelmans et al., 2005). An analysis of the data concerning certificates of tax-deductible gifts handed over to the donors gathered by the Contactgroep Giften (2002) shows that in 1999 'development cooperation' received almost half (48%) of the gifts for which certificates were handed over to natural persons as well as corporations, followed by social services (27%), followed at a long distance by the Red Cross and the King Baudouin Foundation (together 8%), universities (7%) and cultural organizations (5%) (Contactgroep Giften, 2002 – *own calculations*). A study on public support to development cooperation (natural persons only) (Pollet & Huybrechts, 2007) shows that in 2007, 58% of the respondents indicated having donated money in support of development cooperation. This percentage corresponds closely to the percentage in 1990.

Mortelmans et al. (2005: 24) observed that the profile of the Flemish giver is highly similar to that in other countries: older people, and people with higher education and higher incomes are more likely to give. Gender, on the other hand, proved to be an exception. In Flanders, in the year 1999, no gender differences occurred with regard to charitable giving.

Both Damen et al. (2000) and Pollet and Huybrechts (2007) concluded that among the Flemish population, no rational giving strategy existed. Charitable giving is more an impulsive act than a matter of rational planning and calculation. For example, in 2004, 63.3% donated as a result of a campaign (Pollet & Huybrechts, 2007). And in 1999, about half of the sample did not follow any strategy for charitable giving (e.g., budget planning or consciously dividing the available budget across causes and organizations) (Damen et al., 2000). Interestingly, the higher the amount of money donated, the more rational the strategy of giving became: of respondents donating less than 25 euros, 74.2% indicated not having followed any strategy, versus 25% of respondents who donated more than 250 euros and who did follow a strategy (Damen et al., 2000). In addition, the higher the amount of money donated, the more likely the respondents were to donate money via a bank transaction and to deduct their gifts from taxes. The lower the amount of money donated, on the other hand, the more often respondents had bought something tangible in return for their gift.

References

Contactgroep Giften (2002). Rapport betreffende de erkenning van organisaties met het oog op het uitreiken van attesten voor de belastingaftrek van giften in geld. Brussels: Federal Government, Department of Finance. Retrieved July 26, 2008 from http://fiscus.fgov.be/interfaoifnl/Giften/rapport%20Nl.pdf

Damen, S., Mortelmans, D., Raeymaeckers, L., Röben, R., & Versweyveld, D. (2000). *De wilde weldoener? Vlaamse geefpatronen aan liefdadigheid. PSW-paper 2000/8.* Antwerpen: Universiteit Antwerpen.

Federale Overheidsdienst Financiën Retrieved February 11, 2009, from http://fiscus.fgov.be/interfaoifnl/Giften/Instellingen/inleiding.htm#instellingeninwet

Mortelmans, D., Damen, S., & Sinardet, D. (2005). *Lief, liever, ... liefdadig? Over het liefdadigheidsgehalte van de Vlaming. PWS-paper 2005/8.* Antwerpen: Universiteit van Antwerpen.

Pollet, I., & Develtere, P. (2003). *Draagvlak ontwikkelingssamenwerking in Vlaanderen. Resultaten van de enquête in 2003.* Leuven: HIVA.

Pollet, I., & Develtere, P. (2004). *Draagvlak ontwikkelingssamenwerking in Vlaanderen. Resultaten van de enquête in 2004.* Leuven: HIVA.

Pollet, I., & Huybrechts, A. (2007). *Draagvlak ontwikkelingssamenwerking in Vlaanderen. Resultaten van de enquête in 2007.* Leuven: HIVA.

Van Ootegem, L. (Ed.) (1993). *De markt van de vrijgevigheid. Giften in Vlaanderen doorgelicht.* Leuven: Acco

2.3 Czech Republic

Andreas Ortmann[6] and Katarina Svitkova[7]

Data on giving in the Czech Republic are collected by the Czech Statistical Office. The annual reports on nonprofit organizations include also the information on "Contributions and gifts received", as a subcategory of "Other revenues" of nonprofits. The data are presented only in aggregate, as specified in detail below. In 2002, the Czech Statistical Office adopted a new methodology to monitor volunteering, and the data are also available in aggregate in the annual reports on nonprofits (www.czso.cz). These data are reported by nonprofit organizations, i.e. the receiving party.

Data on giving and philanthropic behaviour from donors are not collected on a regular basis and are, therefore, available to a limited extent typically from ad hoc surveys conducted by market research companies at the request of local nonprofits.

A summary of giving data is available at the main information portal for nonprofits in the CR (www.neziskovky.cz). The main surveys conducted in the last 5 years have been: surveys performed by a market research company STEM in 2004 and 2006 for NROS, the Foundation for Development of Civil Society; a survey focused on environmental organizations conducted in 2003 by Nadace Partnerstvi, of the foundation Partnership; a survey of Market Vision for Spiralis in 2003; and surveys by Factum Invenio for the Czech office of UNICEF in 2004, 2005, and 2006. The last survey in 2006 was extended for additional questions in a survey conducted by Factum Invenio without the participation of UNICEF (www.neziskovky.cz).

Corporate philanthropy is promoted mainly by Donors Forum (DF), a nonprofit organization aimed at the development of philanthropy in the country (Donors Forum), and Business Leaders Forum (BLF), a nonprofit organization focused on the promotion of corporate social responsibility (CSR) (Business Leaders Forum). Neither of these organizations, however, conducts regular surveys of corporate giving. BLF performs ad hoc surveys focused on CSR topics: In 2004, they prepared a study on CSR in the Czech Republic, supplemented by a survey. In 2007, they conducted a survey of small and medium-sized enterprises in Prague, focused on their knowledge and usage of CSR.

[6] Andreas Ortmann, CERGE-EI, Charles University and Academy of Sciences of the CR, Center for Design Economics, Prague, Czech Republic, andreas.ortmann@cerge-ei.cz, +420 224 005 117
[7] Katarina Svitkova, Anglo-American University, Prague, Czech Republic, katarina.svitkova@aauni.edu, +420 257 286 627

The data on donations are included also in the tax reports as donations in the Czech Republic are tax-deductible for both individuals and corporations. However because of the Czech privacy laws, it is not possible to obtain individual data from these reports.

The Czech Republic was the first country to introduce the DMS, Donors Message Service (Dárcovská DMS). DMS is an easy way to donate money to philanthropic organizations. The donor sends an SMS to a specific phone number, the SMS costs 30CZK, of which 27CZK is a donation to the chosen nonprofit organization or philanthropic project. The project was initiated by Donors Forum, and gained significant popularity in the country as well as abroad. Its importance in the Czech Republic is illustrated also by the fact that donations given via DMS were exempt from VAT in 2006. Donations via DMS are easy to measure; the results are available at Donors Forum.

Data on nonprofits

The main sources of data on nonprofits are: the Czech Statistical Office, the CVNS (Center for Nonprofit Sector Research), and the public registers of nonprofits administered by ministries or courts.

The Czech Statistical Office (CSO)

- Collects data on nonprofits in periodic surveys

- Is in the process of introducing Satellite Accounts for Nonprofits, which should improve the quality of data and better reflect the actual situation

The CSO annually collected data on nonprofit organizations, sector S15. S15 includes the following nonprofit organizations: associations, clubs, trade unions, political parties, religious organizations, foundations, foundation funds, publicly beneficial organizations, schools and related entities (except public universities), trade associations and chambers, healthcare organizations, associations of home-owners, and associations of hunters. Thus, S15 is broadly defined.

Data for the S15 organizations are collected in two ways: for the organizations with less than 20 employees, which comprises the majority of the sample (around 100,000 entities), the data are collected using questionnaires sent to a random selection of organizations (approx. 10%) and the data were statistically computed for the whole sample. Organizations with more than 20 employees were all contacted via the questionnaires.

Data are available for the period 2002-2006. Data include: number of entities, number of employees, wages (total expenditures on wages), income, costs, assets, property ownership, members, and volunteers. All data are aggregate, individual data are not available. According to Czech legislation, to receive the individual data, the relevant organizations would have to agree with the provision of the information.

The CSO is working on the introduction of a "Satellite Account" for nonprofit organizations. The Satellite Account is being adopted[8] to improve the quality of data on nonprofit organizations and to facilitate international comparisons. One of the main shortcomings of the existing system has been that the CSO collected data on S15 organizations, *Nonprofits serving households*, and these data were presented as 'the nonprofit sector in the Czech Republic'. However, this category does not include all nonprofit organizations. The missing entities are included in the sector of financial and non-financial institutions (entities that were established by, or provide services to, financial or non-financial institutions, and entities with more than 50% of revenues stemming from profit-making activities), governmental institutions (entities where the state provides funding for more than 50% of their expenditures, and public universities), and households. With the adoption of the Satellite Account, the CSO wishes to include also the nonprofit entities from these remaining sectors to the reports on nonprofit organizations.

Another important change brought about with the introduction of the Satellite Account is a better reporting of volunteers and their contribution to the nonprofit sector. With this improved estimation of the volunteers' contribution, it is possible to get a better picture of the size of the nonprofit sector and philanthropic activity in the Czech Republic.

Public registers
NPOs have to register at their establishment either at the courts, with the Ministry of the Interior, the Ministry of Justice, or the Ministry of Culture. A general register of nonprofits is maintained at the Ministry of the Interior.
A general register of nonprofit organizations was established by the Ministry of Informatics in 2006 and is maintained by the Ministry of the Interior (www.isnno.cz). Participation is voluntary, data in the database are self-reported by the nonprofits, and the organizations themselves are responsible for their quality. According to the website, register's administration verifies the submitted data, it is difficult to assess to what extent they manage to do this.

The register contains administrative information (official name, legal form, identification number of the legal entity, year of establishment), information about the activities (mission, field of focus, target group),

---

[8] The Czech Statistical Office agreed to adopt the Satellite Account for Nonprofit Organizations in 2003 as recommended by the Statistical Office of the OSN. CVNS has been the main advisor in the process, facilitating the communication with representatives of the nonprofit organizations in the Czech Republic.

contact information, and information about statutory bodies (CEO, director of the board of trustees). The organizations may disclose additional information or upload relevant documents (e.g. annual reports).

Foundations and foundations funds register at local courts, and are required to file their annual reports there. Filing of annual reports occurs too infrequently, as identified by CVNS in their study of foundations and foundation funds.

Publicly beneficial organizations register at the local courts. The register is available at the Ministry of Justice (Ministry of Justice). The register includes information about the founders of the organization, the date of establishment, and the area in which the charity operates. Publicly beneficial organizations are also required to file their annual reports. The number of annual reports available in the system is, however, very low and therefore provides only limited information about this group of nonprofits.

Religious organizations are registered at the Ministry of Culture. However, there is little information available, and the information that is available mainly concerns the amount of support from public sources (Pospisil, 2005).

Civic associations are registered at the Ministry of the Interior; the register contains only the name and address of the association. According to law, associations are obliged to inform the Ministry when they cease operating. However, because there are no valid incentives to do so, this is seldom done. The register therefore includes a significant number of organizations that no longer exist.

Political parties are registered at the Ministry of the Interior and are required to file their annual report at the Ministry. According to the study of CVNS, 71 of 90 political parties and movements submitted their 2004 annual report to the Ministry.

The CVNS

One of the projects of the CVNS was to evaluate the availability and quality of data on Czech nonprofits. The project started in 2005, and the identified data sources were used to obtain data for the main project of the organization, "Economics of nonprofit organizations in the Czech Republic". The main goal of this project was to study the Czech nonprofit sector, and the analysis was performed separately for different legal entities of the sector. The following types of nonprofits were included:

• Foundations and foundation-like organizations

• Publicly beneficial organizations

• Political parties and movements

• Religious organizations

- Civic associations

- NPOs in education

- Selected other legal forms of nonprofits

The reports provide summary statistics and descriptions of the quality of sources for these organizations. Individual data are available to a limited extent at the CVNS, the availability depending on the methodology of research in the particular group of organizations (i.e., if there was a questionnaire or annual report). In some cases, e.g. the civic associations, the analysis is based solely on the data provided by the Czech Statistical Office (CVNS).

Catalogue of nonprofits
A local internet portal for nonprofit organizations, www.neziskovky.cz, operates a catalogue of nonprofit organizations on its website. Participation is voluntary, nonprofits that want to be included in the catalogue have to register through the website and provide the required information. Thus, the catalogue serves mainly as a marketing tool; all the data are self-reported and are of a qualitative nature (contact details, description of activities, areas of focus). The catalogue is linked to the official register of nonprofits, and there is an indication as to whether the organization is registered in the official register.

References
Business Leaders Forum. Retrieved February 11, 2009, from www.blf.cz
CVNS. Retrieved February 11, 2009, from http://www.e-cvns.cz/en/?stranka=publications&podstranka=1_reports_and_books
Czech Statistical Office. Retrieved February 11, 2009, from http://www.czso.cz/
Dárcovská DMS. Retrieved February 11, 2009, from www.darcovskasms.cz
Donors Forum. Retrieved February 11, 2009, from www.donorsforum.cz
isnno.cz. Retrieved February 11, 2009, from http://www.isnno.cz/evidencennov10001/DesignPages/oevidenci.aspx
Ministry of Justice. Retrieved February 11, 2009, from www.justice.cz
Neziskovky.cz.. Retrieved February 11, 2009, from http://neziskovky.cz/cz/fakta/darcovstvi/darcovstvi-v-cislech/
Neziskovky.cz. Retrieved February 11, 2009, from http://neziskovky.cz/cz/fakta/zpravodajstvi/celorepublikove-akce/3159.html.
Pospisil, M., (2005). *Mapping the Czech Nonprofit Sector*, CVNS.

2.4 France
Antoine Vaccaro[9], Chris Olivier[10] and Edith Bruder[11]

Data sources for household donations in France
There is no overall statistical source in France that provides general data on charitable giving.

First of all, at the State level, information on charitable giving can be derived from tax records on charitable deductions from the French taxation authorities, *the Direction Générale des Finances Publiques.* These data correspond to the donations declared by households living in metropolitan France, overseas departments and territories, and foreign countries.

The *Direction Générale des Finances Publiques* provides three types of data:

- Number of households and amounts donated by department and commune
- Breakdown by tax-liable income brackets of the number of giving households
- Percentage of households that declare donations and average taxable income for the two previous years

  Undeclared donations are evaluated for 2006 at €650 million, compared with €1,575 million declared for the same year. This evaluation was made by comparing fiscal data with the data obtained from a sample of associations about the donations they receive. Undeclared donations are mainly donations in kind and in cash and legacies.

Secondly, since 1999, a population survey has been initiated by *Fondation de France*. Every two or three years, this sample survey carried out by TNS Sofres has collected data on the giving habits of 2,000 randomly selected adults (18 years of age or over). This survey concerns donations in kind, in time, in money (checks, bank transfers, cash, direct debit or generous purchasing), made by individual donors. Respondents were questioned using in-home face-to-face interviews.

The *Direction Générale des Finances Publiques* data have been analyzed by the *Centre d'Etude et de Recherche sur la Philanthropie* (CerPhi - Centre for the Study

[9] Antoine Vaccaro, Centre d'Etude et de Recherche sur la Philanthropie, Paris, France, avaccaro@cerphi.org, + 33 6 15199406

[10] Chris Olivier, Centre d'Etude et de Recherche sur la Philanthropie, Paris, France, chris.olivier@cerphi.org, + 33 6 09787016

[11] Edith Bruder, Centre d'Etude et de Recherche sur la Philanthropie, Paris, France, edith.bruder@cerphi.org + 33 6 14029303

and Research on Philanthropy) since 2004. These data were previously analyzed (from 1993 till 2003) by *Fondation de France*.

Table 2.4.1 Strengths and weaknesses of the French data sources

Strengths	Weaknesses
Administration of tax records	
• Longitudinal data	• In-kind and cash donations are not included (nearly 30%)
• Reliable data: Real figures (not estimates)	• Data obtained with a delay of 2 years
• Data of the total amount of tax-declared donations (vs. randomed estimations)	
• Follow-up available for more than 15 years	
Fondation de France	
• Regularly collected	• Data derived from a panel of French population different from the profile of donators (i.e. over-representation of people more than 50 years old and high socio-economic background)
• Full information on all kinds of giving (cash and in-kind donations)	• There is a possibility that the respondents tend to "overestimate" the size and importance of their charitable activities

Descriptive Statistics

Fiscal context: the deductibility rates of charitable giving in France have increased from 1995 to 2006. For donations to organizations of general interest, the deductibility evolved from 40% of the gift with a maximum of 5% of the income in 1995, to 60% with a maximum of 20% of the income in 2003, and to 66% of the gift in 2005.

For charitable giving to organizations specialized in social care, the deductibility rate increased from 50% of the donation with a maximum of 1040 French Francs (€158) in 1995, to 66% with a maximum of €414 in 2003, and to 75% with a maximum of €470 in 2005.

Since 1995, an analysis of the data shows that the amounts declared by French households have increased from €740 million to €1,575 million in 2006. Between 1995 and 2000, the annual average increase of the amount of declared charitable gifts was about 5%. The years 2001 and 2002 showed very high progressions (11 to 12%). After a break in 2003 (progression comparable to inflation), the increase of declared giving was high in 2004 (19.5%) as a result of new favorable fiscal deductions (August 1st, 2003) and of the donations dedicated to the Tsunami victims (the donations of January 2005 were fiscally deductible from the incomes of 2004). The analysis of the data shows that in 2005, the increase of declared giving rose slightly (5.1 %) and that the year 2006 was stable.

The giving declared in 2007 (2006 incomes) amounted to €1,575 million, compared with €1,555 million the previous year, indicating a slight increase of 1.3%.

From 2005 to 2006, the analysis of the data shows:

- an increase of the donations of people with high incomes, and a decrease of those of low income people. The donations increased by 31% from households with an income over €35,000, and dropped by 22% from households with an income below €35,000. This is true for all income brackets below this threshold.

- the progression of two age brackets of donors: +4.38% of young people of less than 30 years of age (probably as a result of massive recruiting through street fundraising); +5.05% of people between 60 and 69 years of age as a group plausibly less affected by the first pressures on purchasing power.

The number of declaring households increased from 3,893,000 in 1995 to 5,168,869 in 2006. While the annual increase of the declaring households was between 2 and 4% per year from 2000 to 2003, an increase of 15% was recorded in 2004. Between 2005 and 2006 the number of declaring households decreased from 5,361,756 to 5,168,869, which is a fall of 4%.

During the same period, the number of fiscal households has increased. This means that the ratio of donating households to fiscal households therefore decreased by 5%. This fall was distributed differently according to age and income brackets

- The decrease is higher among those under 50 years of age (-9% average)

- The decrease is also higher among the more modest households. The number of declaring households with an income of less than €15,000 decreased by 20%, but taking into account the increase of the number of households belonging to this income bracket, the percentage of donating households decreased by 45%.

- The households with an income from €15,001 to €40,000 show an increase of nearly 40%. The percentage of donating households for this income bracket increased by 12% in 2006.

The average donation increased from €190 in 1995 to €305 in 2006. The progression was relatively low up to 2001, then showed a high increase between 2001 and 2002 (+20%) and again in 2004 and 2005.

From 2005 to 2006, the average donation increased by nearly 5% with important disparities according to age, +10% to 13% for those below 30, less than 5% for those above 60.

Over the last ten years, French charitable giving has been strongly encouraged, legally and fiscally. However, the private financial resources of organizations and foundations do not seem to increase significantly. This is probably due to

- A culture of "Welfare state" turning to "State management", that delegates the support of general interest to the State
- Social and tax contributions that are among the highest worldwide, reinforcing the idea that the State bears responsibility for major social issues (Aberhard et al. 2007; Vaccaro, 1999; 2007).

References

Aberhard, P., Vaccaro, A. & Jedidi S. (2007). *La liberté des ONG humanitaires au risque de leur financement,*. Les éditions hospitalières.

Vaccaro, A. (1999). *International Fund Raising for Not-for-profits: A Country-by-Country Profile.* In T. Harris (Ed.) New York : The AFP/Wiley Fund Development Series.

Vaccaro, A. (2007). *Aspects anthropologiques de la philanthropie et état des lieux de la philanthropie et du mécénat en France.* In Rapport Mondial sur l'argent dans le monde. Association d'économie financière.

2.5 Germany
Burkhard Wilke[12]

Who donates how much, for what purpose, and why? Germany does not yet have a central institution which could provide comprehensive information on the donation activities of the German population. The knowledge about financial and material donations (in contrast to time donations) is generally lacking, although for some years now several studies on this subject have been produced. Frequently, however, these studies are limited to exploring only single aspects and special forms of donation behaviour or certain data on donation volume.

Within the framework of the project "Donations and their Collection in Germany" Priller and Sommerfeld tested and analyzed all data sources obtainable on individual donations from the population. Moreover, they developed a concept for a donation report for Germany (including other kinds of donations like donations from enterprises and legacies). According to Priller/Sommerfeld, information on citizens' donation activities can be gathered from three different sources: official statistics, data from charities and donors – via documentation centers and commercial polls, and indications based on other sources and approaches. The above-mentioned project could function as the starting point for "Giving Germany".

Federal Statistical Office

Continuous Household Budget Surveys and Sample Survey of Income and Expenditure

Within the framework of its household budget surveys, the Federal Statistical Office collects data on income and expenditure, housing conditions, and the possession of durable consumer goods. The Continuous Household Budget Surveys (LWR) annually recorded 6,000 households from 1999 - 2004, and since 2005 the number of households recorded has been 8,000. Households with a monthly net household income of 18,000 euros and over are not included. The Sample Survey of Income and Expenditure (EVS) is conducted once in five years and collects data on the same subjects from 60,000 households.

These household budget surveys also supply information on donations, showing the amounts of donations and membership fees which go to nonprofit organizations. According to the LWR, 4.4 billion euros were

---

[12] Burkhard Wilke, Deutsches Zentralinstitut für soziale Fragen (DZI), Berlin, Deutschland, wilke@dzi.de , +49 30 839001-11

donated to nonprofit organizations, and 6.7 billion euros were spent on membership fees in 2005.

Tax records from the Federal Statistical Office

The Federal Statistical Office has provided specific information on charitable giving by households in Germany since 2001. In 2005, German households deducted a total of 3.1 billion euros from taxes, not taking into account households with a monthly net household income exceeding the ceiling.

Commercial poll data from TNS Infratest

For thirteen years now, TNS Infratest (Taylor Nelson Sofres Polling) has been conducting a monitoring study on household spending, including some questions on charitable giving by individuals. Within this study, 4,000 individuals are asked annually to answer questions concerning their financial expenditures. According to the results, it is estimated that the Germans donated 2.8 billion euros to charitable organizations in 2007.

Commercial poll data from GFK Panel Services Deutschland

GFK compiles the "Charity Scope", a commercial product developed for nonprofit organizations in Germany. The Charity Scope is based on a survey of 10,000 households, using monthly questionnaires. Based on these. it is estimated that German households donated 2.8 billion euros to charitable organizations in 2004/5.

The Donations Almanac issued by the German Central Institute for Social Issues (DZI)

The annually published Donations Almanac contains data on 236 charitable organizations in Germany. These data show that the organizations in question received a total of 1.4 billion euros in 2008. It can thus be estimated in 2008 the sum collected by all the social charitable organizations in Germany amounted to 2,45 billion euros. The estimations on the overall annual donation amount in Germany are between 3 and 5 billion euros."

The DZI study "Evaluation of the new German Donation and Public Benefit Law"

In Summer 2009 the German Central Institute for Social Issues (DZI) will complete a study on the impacts and outcomes of the new German Donation and Public Benefit Law which has been confirmed by the German Parliament in September 2007 and put into practice – backwards – by 1st January 2007. The study has been commissioned by the Federal Ministry of Finance. The study could provide substantial information to be used in a first German Donation Report.

References
Priller, E. & Sommerfeld, J. (2005). Wer spendet in Deutschland? Eine
   sozialstrukturelle Analyse. Discussion Paper. Wissenschaftszentrum
   Berlin für Sozialforschung (WZB)
Priller, E. & Sommerfeld, J. (2009) (eds.): Spenden in Deutschland –
   Analysen, Konzepte, Perspektiven. LitVerlag (forthcoming).

2.6 Hungary
Klára Czike[13] *and Éva Kuti*[14]

Data sources for individual donations in Hungary
Two different sources of empirical information on individual charitable giving are available in Hungary. Both the Hungarian Central Statistical Office (HCSO) and some nonprofit organisations have been involved in the data collection for the last 15 years.

First of all, the HCSO has been carrying out an annual survey of nonprofit organisations since 1993. Its questionnaire includes detailed questions on the components of revenue sources, including a separate item of individual donations. As a result, not only a time-series of the overall amount of individual donations is available, but the breakdown of this amount (by types and size of nonprofit organisations, fields of activities, regions, etc.) can also be analysed on the basis of statistical data (HCSO, 1995–2008).

Secondly, a population survey was initiated by the Nonprofit Kutatócsoport Egyesület (Association for Nonprofit Research) and carried out in partnership with the Hungarian Central Statistical Office (Czakó et al, 1995). This sample survey collected data on the giving habits and voluntary activities of 14,833, randomly selected adults (18 years of age or over) in 1993. Respondents were questioned using the in-home personal interview technique. The questionnaire was broadly similar to those of several other European and North American research projects. The respondents were regarded as individual donors if they supported foundations, voluntary associations, churches, public institutions or private persons other than their family members, relatives and close friends.

A follow-up survey of 5,000 randomly selected Hungarian citizens (14 years of age or over) was conducted in 2004, using almost the same questionnaire. This second survey was the result of the co-operation between the Önkéntes Központ Alapítvány (National Volunteer Centre Foundation) and the Nonprofit Kutatócsoport Egyesület (Czike and Kuti, 2006).

[13] Klára Czike, President of the Board of the Hungarian Volunteer Centre
KAI Consulting Kft. , Budapest, Hungary, czike.klara@kaiconsulting.hu, +36 30 475 8567
[14] Éva Kuti, Budapest College of Management, Budapest, Hungary, kuti.eva@avf.hu, +36 13818118

Table 2.6.1 Strengths and weaknesses of the Hungarian data sources

Strengths	Weaknesses

Statistical survey of nonprofit organisations

• Regularly collected (with the exception of 2001, 2002 and 2004) annual data	• In-kind donations are not included in the figures of individual donations
• All nonprofit organisations receive the questionnaire	• Only about 70% of questionnaires are returned
• Methodologically sophisticated sector-wide estimation of the total amount of individual donations to secular nonprofit organisations	• There is no information on the gifts to private persons, to churches and public organisations

Population surveys of individual giving and voluntary activities

• Representative sample surveys, relatively large sample size	• Long periods between the surveys
• Full information on all kinds of giving (cash and in-kind donations to any types of organisations, giving through purchasing goods, street collections, media campaigns, etc.)	• Difficulties of identifying which of the gifts are received by nonprofit organisations in the case of street collections, donations lines, premium rate text messages, etc.
• Comprehensive profile of the donors (demographic and socio-economic characteristics, social networks, motives for giving)	• Possible bias since the respondents tend to "overestimate" the size and importance of their charitable activities
• "Why not" questions to non-givers	

Descriptive statistics
According to the results of the last sample survey, in 2004 nearly four-fifths of the population aged fourteen and over were involved in making at least one kind of donation out of the following: financial donations, donations in kind, unpaid voluntary activities, and blood donations. This means that almost 7 million people did something, even if it was on a small scale, for the sake of their wider community. Most of them helped people and various nonprofit, governmental, and local governmental institutions, denominations and parties outside their circle of family and friends in more than one way.

In 2004, the most popular form of donations was financial donations. Two-thirds of the population aged 14 or over donated money. The percentage of donors of in kind donations was nearly 50%. The comparison of the results of the surveys of 1993 and 2004 indicate significant growth:

- The percentage of donors of different forms of donations rose from 51 to 68 percent between 1993 and 2004. The share of adults who made monetary donations was 45 and 65 percent, respectively. This growth is probably explained by the fact that the Hungarian nonprofit sector has been extended considerably since 1993. The number of organisations asking for support has also multiplied, as have the opportunities for offering help.

- The percentage of donors making donations only occasionally has dropped and the percentage of donors making regular donations has grown within in-kind donors. The reverse has happened in the case of financial donors, probably due to the proliferation of occasional collections

- Citizens' support preferences have slightly changed over the last decade. Nonprofit organisations specialised in health and social care have a bigger share of the donations than before. Most donors and the largest amount of donations are attracted by churches. The major recipients among secular nonprofit organisations are those working in the field of education, health care, and social care. The support given to cultural, sport, and leisure organisations is also sizable. The rest of the fields can only expect an insignificant percentage of citizens to make donations.

- The socio-demographic composition of supporters has not changed since 1993. The best donors are the middle-aged, married or co-habiting, educated people with 2 or 3 children at the most, high social statuses and are members of civil organisations. Within this group, women participate more in making donations. The influential role of commitment to the church on charitable behaviour has grown perceptibly.

- The number of people emphasising the individual's responsibility for the community is growing. More than half of the donors intend to help people in need by making a donation. More than a third of the donors say that their donation serves the general interest of their community. Only a fraction of the donors refer to their own interest.

The regularly published statistical figures also reflect a significant growth of individual donations to nonprofit organisations:

Table 2.6.2 Secular nonprofit organisations' revenues from individual
donations by fields of activity in Hungary, 1993–2006 (Million HUF)

Year	Education & research	Health & social care	Culture & religion*	Sports & recreation	Other	Total
1993	751.4	530.4	530.3	411.2	346.2	2,569.5
1994	983.7	848.7	795.0	323.2	477.8	3,428.4
1995	1,403.8	1,020.3	950.3	422.1	534.6	4,331.1
1996	1,896.5	1,546.6	1,310.9	666.7	603.0	6,023.7
1997	2,388.1	1,390.9	1,436.3	576.9	776.6	6,568.8
1998	2,434.1	1,859.0	1,595.8	639.3	744.4	7,272.6
1999	2,832.1	2,948.7	1,800.9	716.0	792.0	9,089.7
2000	3,093.8	3,196.8	2,545.3	785.0	1,547.8	11,168.7
2003	3,829.1	3,302.4	2,586.2	1,321.9	2,202.3	13,241.9
2005	5,218.0	5,160.2	2,253.2	1,651.9	2,638.6	16,921.9
2006	6,091.1	5,400.6	3,523.3	2,462.5	2,729.6	20,207.1

* Faith-based charities are included, but churches are not.
Sources: HCSO (1995–2008)

References

Czakó, Á., Harsányi, L., Kuti, É. & Vajda, Á. (1995). Individual giving and
volunteering Központi Statisztikai Hivatal & Nonprofit Kutatócsoport
Egyesület, Budapest. (www.nonprofitkutatas.hu)

Czike, K. & Kuti, É. (2006). Önkéntesség, jótékonyság, társadalmi integráció
(Volunteering, charity, social integration). Nonprofit Kutatócsoport
Egyesület,   Önkéntes   Központ   Alapítvány,   Budapest.
(www.nonprofitkutatas.hu)

HCSO (1995–2008). Nonprofit szervezetek Magyarországon, 1993, 1994,
1995, 1996, 1997, 1998, 1999, 2000, 2003, 2005, 2006 (Nonprofit
organisations in Hungary, 1993, 1994, 1995, 1996, 1997, 1998, 1999,
2000, 2003, 2005, 2006), Központi Statisztikai Hivatal, Budapest.

Kuti, É. (2002). Individual charitable giving and volunteering in Hungary. In:
Abramson, Alan J. (ed.): *Mapping new worlds. Selected research on the nonprofit
sector around the globe*, The Aspen Institute, Washington, DC.

Kuti, É. & Czike, K. (2005). Citizens' Donations and Voluntary Activities
(Flash report on the findings of the 2004 survey) (www.onkentes.hu).

2.7 Ireland
Geraldine Prizeman[15] and Andrew O'Regan[16]

Introduction
Research on philanthropic giving in Ireland is limited to a small number of discrete studies with poor comparability. On a more positive note a number of recent State and private initiatives are seeking to place philanthropy on the public agenda. In this context the lack of comprehensive and longitudinal data is increasingly recognised as problematic and attention is turning to how this might be addressed. In this chapter a brief introduction to the historical and legal context in Ireland is provided first before consideration in given to the main studies in the field.

Historical context
The tradition of giving is rooted in a Christian ethos which has hugely influenced the behaviour of individuals in Irish society since early medieval times (National Committee on Volunteering 2002). From the 18th Century religious institutions began to take a role in the provision of social services, particularly in the area of healthcare and education (Ruddle and Mulvihill 1995). Following political independence in 1922 the establishment of many charitable organisations continued to be influenced by the Christian teaching and the Roman Catholic concern with subsidiarity (Ruddle and Mulvihill 1995, Donnelly-Cox and Jaffro 1999). In this context the message of giving was (and still is) reinforced within schools and within the Churches. Other streams of nonprofit organisation formation in the late 19th and early 20th centuries, such as rural regeneration, community development and rights based organisations, have also benefited from this orientation towards giving.

In recent times Ireland has experienced a period of economic growth which has improved the economic status of many individuals. While it has been suggested that this economic growth has increased the potential for charitable giving in Ireland (Donoghue, O'Regan, McGee and Donovan 2007), there is no empirical evidence that this potential has been realised. Indeed the average household donation as a percentage of disposable income has decreased over this period (Central Statistics Office 1996, 2001, 2006).

---

[15] Geraldine Prizeman, Centre for Nonprofit Management, School of Business, Trinity College Dublin 2, Dublin, Ireland, prizemag@tcd.ie, +353 1 896 3230
[16] Andrew O'Regan, Centre for Nonprofit Management, School of Business, Trinity College Dublin 2, Dublin, Ireland, aoregan@tcd.ie, +353 1 896 2631

Legal context

In Ireland at present, until the enactment of legislation[17], there is no one legal status for nonprofit organisations, there are however, a number of structures adopted by organisations which include; a company limited by guarantee with no shareholders, Industrial Provident Society, a friendly society, a charitable trust, an incorporated body and an unincorporated association (Law Society of Ireland 2002; Acheson, Harvey, Kearney and Williamson 2004). This lack of a clear legislative framework means that there is no single register of nonprofit organisations.

The Office of the Revenue Commissioners, Charities Section maintains a database of nonprofit organisations[18] to which they have granted charitable tax exemption on the grounds that they are constituted and operate exclusively for charitable purposes. Qualifying charitable purposes are defined under English and Irish case law and under *Income Tax Special Purposes Commissioners vs. Pemsel* (1893) (Acheson *et al.* 2004; Office of the Revenue Commissioners 2005). Statistical data about corporate or individual giving to these organisations is not gathered by The Revenue Commissioners.

In the absence of a single legal identifier, the most commonly-used term by both practitioners and the government in Ireland is 'voluntary and community organisations' (Hayes 1996; Donoghue 1998; Donnelly-Cox and Jaffro 1999; Department of Social, Community and Family Affairs 2000). A recent study on nonprofit organisations in Ireland reported that almost four in ten organisations referred to themselves as a 'community' organisation with a further 30 per cent stating that they were a 'voluntary' organisation and only 6 per cent of organisations referred to themselves as a 'charity'. (Donoghue, O'Regan, Prizeman and Nöel 2006)

Data sources for individual giving in Ireland

There is no one statistical source for data on giving to nonprofit organisations in Ireland at the moment. Over the years a number of sources have provided data on individual donations[19].

---

[17] In February 2009 the General Scheme for the Charities Regulation Bill was enacted by the President of Ireland. The Bill provides for a new legal structure for charities and for a Register of Charities to be established (Department of Community, Rural and Gaeltacht Affairs 2009).

[18] The full list of bodies granted exemption is published on the Revenue Commissioners website: www.revenue.ie

[19] Research has been conducted on corporate giving in Ireland (Donoghue 2002) but the focus of this chapter is on individual giving only.

Individual Giving Survey Series

To date the most comprehensive data was collected in series of national studies of individual giving and volunteering, during the 1990's (Ruddle and O'Connor 1993; Ruddle and Mulvihill 1995, 1999). These tracked the extent and nature of donating behaviour over a 12-month period in 1992, 1994 and 1997/98. The first two surveys[20] involved a representative random sample of 1,000 participants who were asked about donating and volunteering behaviour in the month prior to being interviewed. The last survey (data collected in 1995) employed a different methodology with the fieldwork distributed over 12 months from March 1997 to February 1998 and participants recorded the value of all donations made during the month prior to interview in a journal (Ruddle and Mulvihill 1999). In each of the three surveys comprehensive data was collected on the (i) general profile of respondents, (ii) extent and nature of charitable giving; (iii) extent and nature of volunteering; and (iv) general attitudes towards charities and volunteers.

Household Expenditure Surveys

The State's Central Statistics Office gathers data on donations as part of the National Household Budget Survey (HBS). The HBS is a survey of a representative random sample of all private households in the State. First conducted in 1951, the survey has been conducted approximately every five years since[21] (Carroll, McCarthy and Newman 2005). The latest survey (2004-2005) involved 6,884 households (Central Statistics Office 2006). As part of this general survey individuals were asked several questions related to giving to nonprofit organisations. First, individuals were asked to indicate the 'voluntary subscriptions' that were made to schools[22]. This included payments for extra curricular activities such as games and languages. Second, individuals were asked about subscriptions and contributions made to clubs, associations and the church (Central Statistics Office 2006). In addition, diaries were collected from individuals and some data on charitable donations may have been contained in those.

---

[20] Data collected in March 1992 and 1994

[21] Seven large-scale surveys have been undertaken in respect of the periods 1951-52, 1965-66, 1973, 1980, 1987, 1994-95 and 1999-2000. The 1951-52 and the 1965-66 surveys were, however, restricted to urban areas. The 1973, 1980, 1987, 1994-95 and 1999-2000 surveys covered both urban and rural households.

[22] While in Ireland most of schools' funding comes from the State, the responsibility for the running of national schools rests with voluntary Boards of Management (Donoghue 1999).

One-off national surveys
A once-off study was conducted by independent consultants in 2005. In the study 1,000 adults aged between 15 and 74 were consulted about charities and charitable giving in June 2005 (Amárach 2005). Respondents were asked about the areas of charity that people donated to, the methods of donating and the amount donated in a 'typical month'.   To date there has not been any follow-up study.

Organisational surveys
In 2005 a project to map nonprofit organisations in Ireland was undertaken by the Centre for Nonprofit Management (CNM) at the School of Business, Trinity College, Dublin (Donoghue *et al.* 2006). In total 4,214 organisations participated in the study.[23] Data collected about organisational finances in the survey examined the total income from private sources (including, individual donations and foundation support) and provides some idea on the amount of private funding received by nonprofit organisations in Ireland. This survey is distinguishable from others in that data were collected from organisations and not from the individuals who donated. There has been no follow-up study conducted.

Review of the data sources

Table 2.7.1 Strengths and weaknesses of the Irish data sources

Strengths	Weaknesses
Individual Giving Series	
• Longitudinal data dating back to 1992	• Old data as not conducted since 1997/8
• Population results	• Relatively small sample size
• Representative study	• Data on in-kind donations not collected
• Large range of background data collected	
• Data on the motivation for donating collected	
• Comprehensive questionnaire developed for the surveys	
• Data on gross household income (for analysis purposes) collected	
• Publically available results	

[23] The valid total sample size for the survey was 22,331 organisations.

Strengths	Weaknesses
• Data on volunteering trends as well as donating trends collected	

National Household Expenditure Survey

• Longitudinal data dating back to 1951	• Question format means that results are not comparable with other surveys on donating
• Population results	• Only conducted every five years
• Representative study	• Findings not presented in an easily understood format
• Large sample size	• Data on the motivation for donating not collected
• Large range of background data collected	• Data on in-kind donations not collected
• Data linked to other household expenditure	• Data on volunteering not collected
• Large government-funded survey	
• Publically available results	

Once-off National Surveys

• Representative study	• Relatively small sample size
• Population results	• Has not been repeated
• Publically available results	• Findings related to income not presented in report
• Relatively recent data	• Data linked employment status and not level of income
• Data on types of charity donated to collected	• Data on volunteering not collected
• Data on methods of donating collected	• Data on the motivation for donating not collected
	• Data on in-kind donations not collected

Organisational Survey

• Large Sample Size	• Not comparable to other studies as data collected from the organisation as opposed to the individual.
• Representative of nonprofit organisations in Ireland	• Has not been repeated

Strengths	Weaknesses
• Relatively recent data	• Question format means that results are not comparable with other surveys on donating
• Publically available data	
• Data collected using organisational accounts as opposed to individual memory of giving	
• Data on volunteering collected	

Descriptive statistics

This section outlines the headline results from each of the sources and provides a general picture of 'giving' in Ireland.

The Reaching Out Series

The reaching out series refers to a number of national surveys that were conducted in Ireland. The three surveys (1992, 1994 and 1997/8) examined individual donating and volunteering. The donating data from the 1997/8 survey are presented here as there were no significant differences in the data over the series of surveys.

The majority of individuals interviewed (87%) donated money to charity and 79 per cent gave more than once in the previous month. Most of the donations given (86%) were prompted by appeals to donate. Only a small proportion of individuals (8%) gave in any planned way. Taking account of the full sample, the average monthly donation per individual was €9.97. The total amount donated by all adults (using Census data) over the course of the year of the survey was calculated to have been 'somewhere between' €268 and €343 million. The most common modes of donating were (i) the church gate collection (43% of donors); (ii) the street collection/flag day (30% of donors); and (iii) raffle tickets/lines (29% of donors). While the church precinct was the most common locale for donating, only 12 per cent of the total amount donated was given to the church. The greatest beneficiaries of these donations were organisations in the ICNPO fields of social services (29%), health (23%), international activities (13%) and sports and recreation (10%).

While there were no gender differences in propensity to donate, individuals living in rural and town areas donated significantly larger amounts than those in urban areas. Those who attached importance to religion donated significantly more than those for whom religion was unimportant. Donating was positively related to household income, level of education and employment status. Most people indicated that they donated because they deemed it was 'for a good cause' while almost one-third (31%) of donors said that they gave simply because they 'were asked'.

Household Expenditure Surveys

The Household Budget Survey (HBS) is a survey of a representative random sample of all private households in Ireland. The data presented here are derived from the final results from the 2004-2005 HBS and are based on a sample size of 6,884 households. As the survey questions related to contributions made to churches, voluntary schools, charity[24], trade unions/professional associations as well as other sporting clubs and sporting associations it is not clear if all monies captured in the survey are related to individual donations to charities.

The average weekly contribution per individual was €8.94[25]. Contributing behaviour was related to the employment status of individuals as well as their gross income. Those who were unemployed contributed significantly less (€3.05 weekly) than the average weekly contribution (€8.94) while those in employment (€10.58) the self employed (€10.27) and the retired (€9.22) contributed above the weekly average. Those in the higher income deciles contributed nominally more and proportionally less than those in the lower deciles. Individuals with a gross weekly income of less than €190.37 contributed €4.53 per week (2.4 % of gross income) while those with a gross weekly income of more than €2,019.06 contributed €18.19 per week (0.1% of gross income). Church dues[26] were the single greatest recipient of contributions receiving an average weekly contribution of €4.04, almost half the total amount contributed weekly.

Once-off National Survey

The Amárach study (conducted in 2005) estimated that a total of €450 million was donated to charity in Ireland, with €15 being the average monthly amount donated. Individuals were unlikely to donate on a regular

---

[24] It is not clear from the questionnaire and published tables what is implied by the term 'charity'.

[25] By using population data (CSO 2007) we can find an estimate the total amount donated in 2004-2005 as being in the order of €1.5 billion. This sum is considerable larger than other estimates and suggests that the data reported refers not only to charitable donating but to subscriptions paid to other associations and sporting clubs.

[26] 'Church dues' are contributions by members of a parish community towards the defrayment of operational expenses of the parish. While voluntary, they are a customary expression of church membership.

monthly basis, with just 12 per cent doing so. Over half (53%) of individuals donating gave to street collections with 40 per cent donating to sponsored fund-raising drives[27].

Examining the findings across demographic groups the study found that support for health-related charities rose steeply with age while support for children's charities fell as the age categories increased. The inclination to donate to charity appeared to be strongly influenced by gender, age and location. Those who had a third level education and those who were employed were more likely to donate larger amounts than other groups.

Organisational survey
As the focus of this 2006 study was organisational and not individual the data presented here is constituted of organisational reporting of donations received. This data is not directly comparable to the other data presented above as the figures also included donations by private foundations as well as individuals. The data, however, is derived from audited accounts as opposed to individual memory. The data collected on income in the survey was based on 2003 financial figures. In total 3,215 organisations reported on their sources of income. Findings in the study suggested that over half of organisations (52.8%) received some form of private donations which amounted to over €200 million (€200,942,710) (Donoghue *et al.* 2006).

Looking at the kinds of organisations that reported private donations, one quarter (25.1%) were international development organisations while over one fifth (21.6%) were social service organisations. Other kinds of organisations included philanthropy organisations (10.4%); arts, culture and heritage organisations (8.4%); and health organisations (8%). At the lower end of the scale trade unions (0.3%) and environmental organisations (0.6%) were less likely to have had received private donations.

Conclusion
There are a limited and disparate number of sources from where data on individual giving to charities in Ireland can be obtained. Surveys have been conducted on an *ad hoc* basis and have been based on individual and private institutional interest rather than being part of state-funded national data collection strategies. Data that is available to date suggest that a large proportion of Irish people donate to charity and that the amount that individuals donate has increased from €9.97 monthly in 1996 (Ruddle and

---

[27] Sponsored fund-raising drives are where individuals are sponsored to carry out some activity, for example, a parachute jump or walking trek. Monies collected by the sponsored individual are donated to a named charity.

Mulvihill 1997) to €15.00 in 2005 (Amárach 2005). It seems, however, that people do not necessarily donate proportionally based on their income level, and that there is the potential for higher levels of giving in Ireland.

There are many research gaps that need to be filled in relation to philanthropic activity in Ireland. In order to track trends in philanthropic giving, data needs to be gathered in a systematic way using methodologies that include consistent categories (with regard to employment status, income level and other demographic details) so that comparisons can be made across studies and across timelines.

Looking to the future, a considerable role could be played by the Central Statistics Office (CSO) in gathering relevant data. In the most recent Census (data gathered in 2006) data was gathered on levels and kinds of volunteering. In a similar manner data on levels of donating to charities could also be gathered at the same time that other Census data was being collected. The CSO already collect data on giving in their Household Budget Surveys but in a manner that conflates charitable donations with other kinds of contributions. Adjusting the questions asked could provide more accurate figures on individual levels of giving.

Under current legislation, The Charities Act (2009), a Charities Regulatory Authority will be established and all charities in Ireland will be bound to comply with the resulting legal registration and accountability provisions of the Act. This will involve changes for the charities sector in Ireland and could allow for all kinds of data (including philanthropic giving) to be gathered from organisations. It will, however, be some time before any data can be collected from this source and the tracking of trends can take place. Other initiatives that could provide data on giving in the future include the proposal to establish a Guidestar Ireland project[28].

In summary, the state of giving research in Ireland is non-systematic and limited. At the moment it seems that the State is best positioned to gather data that would fill the existing gaps. Without such data our understanding of the philanthropic impact of the relatively recent increase in private disposable income in Ireland will remain very limited.

---

28 GuideStar is an online Web-based directory of nonprofit organisations and utilizes information sources of public disclosure.

References

Acheson, N., Harvey, B., Kearney, J. & Williamson, A. (2004). *Two Paths, One Purpose: Voluntary Action in Ireland, North and South.* Dublin: Institute of Public Administration

Amárach Consulting (2005). *Good Intentions: Consumer Preferences for Charities in Ireland,* Dublin: Amárach Consulting

Carroll, McCarthy & Newman (2005). 'An Econometric Analysis of Charitable Donations in the Republic of Ireland' in *The Economic and Social Review*, Vol. 36, No. 3 pp. 229-249

Central Statistics Office (2007). *Census 2006: Principal Demographic Results*, Dublin: The Stationery Office

Central Statistics Office (1996). *Household Budget Survey 1994-1995: Final Results*, Dublin: The Stationery Office

Central Statistics Office (2001). *Household Budget Survey 1999-2000: Final Results*, Dublin: The Stationery Office

Central Statistics Office (2006). *Household Budget Survey 2004-2005: Final Results*, Dublin: The Stationery Office

Department of Community Rural and Gaeltacht Affairs. (2009).*Charities Act, 2009.*Dublin: The Stationery Office

Department of Social, Community and Family Affairs (2000). *Supporting Voluntary Activity*. Dublin: The Stationery Office.

Donnelly-Cox, G., & Jaffro, G. (1999). *The Voluntary Sector in the Republic of Ireland: into the twenty-first century.* Coleraine: Centre for Voluntary Action Studies.

Donoghue, F. (1998). *Defining the Nonprofit Sector Ireland.* Baltimore: The Johns Hopkins Institute for Policy Studies.

Donoghue, F. (2002). *Philanthropy or Advertising: Corporate Giving to the Nonprofit Sector in Ireland,* Dublin: Policy Research Centre, National College of Ireland

Donoghue, F., Anheier, H.K. & Salamon, L.M. (1999). *Uncovering the Nonprofit Sector in Ireland.* Dublin: Johns Hopkins University/National College of Ireland.

Donoghue, F., O'Regan, A., McGee, S. & Donovan, A.M. (2007). *Exploring the Irish Fundraising Landscape: A Report on the Practice and Scale of Charitable Fundraising from the Public in Ireland,* Dublin: Centre for Nonprofit Management, Trinity College Dublin

Donoghue, F., Prizeman, G., O'Regan, A. & Nöel, V. (2006). *The Hidden Landscape: First Forays into Mapping Nonprofit Organisations in Ireland.* Dublin: Centre for Nonprofit Management, School of Business, Trinity College Dublin

Hayes, T. (1996). *Management, Control and Accountability in Nonprofit/ Voluntary Organisations.* Aldershot: Avebury.

Law Society of Ireland (2002). *Charity Law: The case for reform.* Dublin: Law Society Law Reform Committee.

National Committee on Volunteering (2002). *Tipping the Balance: Report and recommendations to governance on supporting and developing volunteering in Ireland,* Dublin: National Committee on Volunteering

Office of the Revenue Commissioners (2005). *CH1-Applying for Relief from Tax on the Income and Property of Charities. Dublin: Office of the Revenue Commissioners*

Ruddle, H. & Mulvihill, R. (1995). *Reaching Out: Charitable Giving and Volunteering in the Republic of Ireland. The 1994 Survey,* Dublin: Policy Research Centre, National College of Industrial Relations

Ruddle, H and Mulvihill, R. (1999). *Reaching Out: Charitable Giving and Volunteering in the Republic of Ireland. The 1997/98 Survey,* Dublin: Policy Research Centre, National College of Industrial Relations

Ruddle, H and O'Connor, J (1993). *Reaching Out: Charitable Giving and Volunteering in the Republic of Ireland,* Dublin: Policy Research Centre, National College of Industrial Relations

2.8 Italy
Giuliana Gemelli[29]

The state of giving research in Italy is in an early stage. This is basically related to the historical factor of the rather inconsistent work done by statistics national agency ISTAT. As shown in the table reproduced below, there is a substantial lack of well-constructed taxonomies to define the dimension of giving in Italy.

Table 2.8.1 Area of activity of philanthropic institutions

Area of activity	Operating (%)	Grant-making (%)	Mixed (%)	Total (%)
Social Assistance	26.1	-	14.4	17.3
Culture	21.6	-	19.1	16.5
Education	23.4	-	6.3	13.5
Financing Projects	-	37.9	17.2	12.8
Philanthropy	1.4	37.2	15	12.7
Religion	5.3	23.9	3.8	8.5
Research	8.3	-	11.7	7.7
Economic development and social cohesion	5.8	-	4.2	4.2
Health	4	-	2.7	2.8
International cooperation and solidarity	0.3	1.1	2.4	1.1
Sport & recreation	1.7	-	0.8	1
Environment	1.4	-	0.9	1
Unions	0.4	-	1	0.5
Civil rights and political activities	0.3	-	0.3	0.3
Number of foundations	2,338	943	1,439	4,720

In Italy, giving is still considered as an act of benevolence without a specific aim. This is why the category of philanthropy is still defined separately from other patterns of granting at the level of the giving organization. This limit is overwhelmed by the fact that

---

[29] Giuliana Gemelli, Director Master in International Studies in Philanthropy and International Research Center on Philanthropy and Social Innovtion PHaSI, Dipartimento di discipline storiche, University of Bologna, Bologna, Italy, +39 051 2098106 giuliana.gemeli@unibo.it

a- the census has not addressed any specific question about giving at the level of the household.

b- ipso facto we have very poor knowledge about family giving including the organized dimension of family private independent foundations.

The second main relevant aspect is related to the fact that the development of giving organization in Italy (Foundations – both family private and corporate, as well as those originated from bank origins or financial institutions) has a relatively short history. This history started in the late 1980s of the last century. It is a fact that an attempt to strengthen the role of private giving organizations and corporate foundations was made in the mid-sixties with the creation of a small number of American-style grant-making foundations and some important cultural foundations based on family initiatives like the Fondazione Einaudi, the Fondazione Feltrinelli, and the Fondazione Agnelli as well as the Fondazione Adriano Olivetti. All of these are still very important foundations in Italy, with a profile based on mixed activities - operating and grant-making rather than only grant-making which was and still is mainly an operating foundation. Actually, the model of "pure" grant-making foundation did not develop very much in Italy and this includes also both the family and private foundations.

A deeper analysis of this phenomenon in historical perspective reveals that a relevant obstacle vis-à-vis the development of private initiative in giving was related to the dominant role of the Catholic church. Since the fall of the Roman Empire and the beginning of Christianity, the Church has created a quasi monopoly in the assistance and control of the poor. The modern substitute of the foundation in Italy at the end of the 19th century did nothing to change this quasi monopoly since on the one hand they allowed a coordination of the assistance to the poor, but on the other hand exercised political control which benefitted the authoritarian governments until the fascist era.

It is also a matter of fact that family giving during the last century has been more directed towards traditional activities following eleemosynary patterns rather than developing strategic grant-making. In the last twenty years, a growing number of family foundations have been created but this has not affected the giving patterns of Italian citizens very much since most of them prefer to give to the Church rather than to support new and to some extent "risky" initiatives - or initiatives perceived to be risky - originating from civil society.

Foundations in Italy seem to do much and rather better in attracting donations and bequests.

Table 2.8.2 Foundation type and composition of financial sources

Foundation type	Composition of financial sources
Operating (50% of the total)	- 54% from the Italian government (contracts, subsidies and grants) - 30% from sales of products - 3% from the return on capital investments - less than 3% donations or associates contributions
Grant-making (20% of the total)	- 86% from return on capital investments (more than half from foundations originating from banks return on endowments) - 10% from founder contribution - less than 2% from other donations -
Foundation type	Composition of financial sources
Mixed (30% of the total)	- 48.2% from members' fees or associated members' contributions - 18% from the Italian government (mainly contracts, but also earmarks and grants) - 17.3% from return on capital investments - 6.2% from sales of products - less than 5% from other donations

In order to give an idea of the situation of Italian philanthropy, we have collected the key figures from the most recently available studies on the subject. Each component will then be analyzed in separate paragraphs.

Table 2.8.3 Giving in Italy

Foundation giving (2006 survey)	Nearly €4 billion in grants for social purposes[30], compared to a total expenditure of €11.5 billion on the part of both grantmaking and operating foundations *Note*: total expenditure of foundations of originating from banks reached €1.5 billion, of which about 92% went towards grants (and 25% of these grants to NPOs)[31]
Individual donations to NPOs (2005 estimate[32])	Over €4 billion. This includes religiously inspired public benefit organizations, but not alms to the Church or religious congregations. It is estimated that less than 2.5% of this sum consisted of bequests.
Corporate giving (2005 estimate)	€266 million, not including in-kind donations and other sponsorships that are deducted as costs instead of charitable donations.
Cinque per mille - Government allocation of 0,5% of personal income tax (2006 official data)	€395 million. This represents direct contributions from individuals who are free to give their personal share of taxes to their favourite NPO or research institution.

If we compare this to the main US source for similar data – Giving USA 2006 – we see that total giving is about 4-5 times smaller in Italy than in the US, while individual giving is about 6-7 times smaller[33]:

- Foundations $30 billion (11.5% of the total) of which $4 billion from corporate foundations
- Individuals $200 billion (76.5% of the total) + bequests $17 billion (6.7%)
- Corporations $14 billion (5.3% of the total)

The claim that in Italy (as well as in the rest of Europe) the government supports nonprofits much more than in the US is not really true. According to recent studies, income of nonprofit organizations from direct and indirect

[30] ISTAT, Italian National Census Bureau, "First survey on Foundations", result published in November 2007
[31] ACRI , Italian Association of Saving Banks and Bank-origin Fondations, "11th Report"
[32] Source Istituto Ricerca Sociale, IRS http://www.irs-online.it/
[33] This elaboration include the population ratio US-Italy of 6:1 but is biased by exchange rate fluctuations

US governmental sources is estimated to be at least 30%[34] (not including the contributions to faith-based initiatives), a statistic comparable with Italian data, which confirm the income from public sources to be about 35%. In any case, contracts and subsidies from public sources are by and large the main source of income for the tertiary sector, with annual contributions amounting to over €15 billion.

It is always very important to take this quantitative approach to philanthropy if we want to adopt a critical and constructive perspective on what can be realistically achieved in Europe. Government spending on public health alone accounts for about €90 billion, while overall public expenditure is about 50% of the national GDP. Therefore it is obvious that philanthropy – let alone foundations – could never replace the State in the provision of social services. In spite of this, both individual culture and political attention have drastically altered the Italian landscape in the last 15 years. We will continue our analysis by examining the new environment in which Italian foundations function.

What has really changed the scenario is the role of volunteering and the donations not only of money but also of time, skills and intellectual and social capital that circulate through this vehicle, which produce significantly more relevant and large quantities of information and empirical data.

---

[34] Source: NCCS – Urban institute, http://nccs.urban.org/

2.9 The Netherlands
Pamala Wiepking[35]

Data sources for household donations in the Netherlands
The main data source for household donations to charitable organizations in the Netherlands is the Giving in the Netherlands study, conducted by the VU University Amsterdam. In 1993, the Giving in the Netherlands study was initiated by Theo Schuyt, and since then a survey on giving and volunteering by households, companies, charitable organizations, foundations, and charitable lotteries has been conducted every two years.

In 2001, the Giving in the Netherlands study evolved into a bi-annual panel study on household donations, GINPS. GINPS consists of a longitudinal database with information on donations made by approximately 1,400 households. Four waves are currently available: 2001 (GINPS01), 2003 (GINPS03), and 2005 (GINPS05). The fourth wave, GINPS07, has become available in 2009. Another source of information on household donations that recently became available is the Dutch Belastingdienst (Revenue Service). The Dutch Revenue Service provides tax records with information on the charitable deductions used by households.

Table 2.9.1 Strengths and weaknesses of the Dutch data sources

Strengths	Weaknesses
GINPS	
• Longitudinal study	• Low to middle high income range
• Excellent questions on giving (adaptation of 'Method+Area' module)	• Prosocial sample bias (people who participate regularly in survey research)
• Large range of background characteristics	
Tax records	
• Longitudinal data	• Includes only itemizers
• Complete income range	• Small range of background characteristics

---

[35] Pamala Wiepking, Department of Philanthropic Studies, VU University Amsterdam, Amsterdam, the Netherlands, P.Wiepking@fsw.vu.nl, +31 (0)20 598 69 22

Descriptive statistics

Table 2.9.2 shows total household donations (in millions of euros) to different charitable subsectors in the Netherlands, for the period 1995-2005. In 2005, the total amount donated to charitable causes was 1.9 billion euros. Religious organizations (including organizations supporting religious ideology and religious institutions such as churches, mosques, etc.) received the most money. These are followed by organizations active in the international aid sector, organizations active in the health sector, the environment, nature and animal protection sector, and the public and social benefits sector. Recipient organizations receiving the lowest total of donations from Dutch households are organizations active in the fields of education and research, culture, and sports and recreation.

Table 2.9.2 Charitable giving by households in the Netherlands, 1995-2005

Charitable subsector	Household donations (in millions of euros)					
	1995	1997	1999	2001	2003	2005
Religion	574	482	429	694	864	704
International aid	290	229	328	367	304	439
Health	260	136	245	236	283	234
Environment/nature /animals	102	96	128	134	154	158
Public and social benefits	86	83	129	172	142	166
Other (not specified)	42	25	41	69	49	61
Education/research	21	26	21	31	44	33
Culture	13	22	23	33	22	31
Sports/recreation	30	22	70	52	37	29
Total	1,419	1,121	1,414	1,788	1,899	1,854

Source: GINPS05 (2005)

The numbers in table 2.9.2 show that the donations by Dutch households decreased slightly between 2003 and 2005 (though this decrease is not significant). However, overall there was a steady increase in total donations to charitable organizations in the Netherlands in the period between 1995 and 2005.

Table 2.9.3 shows the percentage of households that donate to recipient organizations in different charitable subsectors. It is apparent that most households donate to organizations active in the health sector. Seventy-six percent of the Dutch households donated to health in 2007. Almost half of the Dutch households donated to the environment, nature and animal protection sector. Thirty-eight percent of the Dutch households donated to public and social benefits, which is comparable to the percentage of households that donated to international aid. In the Netherlands, about 45% of the population considers themselves religiously affiliated. Taking this into account, the result that only 30% of the Dutch households donated to religion seems rather meagre. Recipient organizations active in the field of sports and recreation, culture and arts, and education and research receive donations from the lowest percentage of Dutch households.

In addition to the percentage of donors, table 2.9.3 also shows the mean household donation to a particular charitable subsector, calculated using donating households only. On average, Dutch households donate the highest amounts to religious organizations. Recipient organizations in the 'other' category receive the second-highest average donations (in the Netherlands this category also includes service organizations such as the Rotary). Organizations active in the public and social benefits sector receive the lowest average donations.

Table 2.9.3 Percentage households and mean amount donated for donations to different charitable subsectors in the Netherlands in 2007 (*n*=1,777)

	% households that donated	Mean donation among donating households (in euros)
Health	75.8	42.74
Environment/nature/animals	48.2	49.13
Public and social benefits	38.2	23.47
International aid	36.6	68.22
Religion	29.8	351.90
Sports/recreation	14.3	38.09
Culture	9.9	30.81
Education/research	6.2	37.34
Other (not specified)	0.6	112.09
Total	86.1	239.11

Source: GINPS07 (2007)

References

Bekkers, R. & Schuyt, T.N.M. (forthcoming). 'And Who is Your Neighbor? Explaining the Effect of Religion on Charitable Giving and Volunteering.' *Review of Religious Research*.

Bekkers, R. & Wilhelm, M.O. (forthcoming). 'Helping Behavior, Dispositional Empathic Concern, and the Principle of Care'. *Social Psychology Quarterly*.

Bekkers, R. & Bowman, W. (forthcoming). 'The Relationship Between Confidence in Charitable Organizations and Volunteering Revisited'. *Nonprofit and Voluntary Sector Quarterly*.

Bekkers, R. (forthcoming). 'Straight From the Heart'. In: *Advances in Medical Sociology: Patients, Consumers and Civil Society: US and International Perspectives*, edited by Susan Chambré and Melinda Goldner. Emerald Publishing.

Bekkers, R. & Veldhuizen, I. (2008). 'Geographical Differences in Blood Donation and Philanthropy in the Netherlands: What Role for Social Capital?' *Journal of Economic & Social Geography*, 99 (4): 483-496.

Bekkers, R., Völker, B., Van der Gaag, M. & Flap, H.D. (2008). "Social Networks of Participants in Voluntary Associations". In: Lin, N. & B. Erickson (Eds.). *Social Capital: Advances in Research*. Oxford University Press.

Bekkers, R. (2008). 'Volunteerism'. Pp. 641-643 in: Darity, William A. Jr. (Ed.). *International Encyclopedia of the Social Sciences*, 2nd Edition. Detroit: Macmillan Reference USA.

Bekkers, R. (2007). 'Measuring Altruistic Behavior in Surveys: The All-Or-Nothing Dictator Game.' *Survey Research Methods,* 1(3): 139-144.

Bekkers, R. & Wiepking, P. (2007). 'Generosity and Philanthropy: A Literature Review'. Report commissioned by the John Templeton Foundation. Available at SSRN: http://ssrn.com/abstract=1015507.

Bekkers, R. (2007). 'Intergenerational Transmission of Volunteerism.' *Acta Sociologica*, 50 (2): 99-114.

Bekkers, R. & Crutzen, O. (2007). "Just keep it simple: A field experiment on fundraising letters". *International Journal of Nonprofit and Voluntary Sector Marketing*, 12 (4): 371-378.

Bekkers, R. (2006). 'Traditional and Health-Related Philanthropy: The Role of Resources and Personality'. *Social Psychology Quarterly*, 68 (4): 349-366.

Bekkers, R., & Wiepking, P. (2006). 'To Give or Not to Give...That's the Question'. *Nonprofit & Voluntary Sector Quarterly*, 35 (3): 533-540.

Bekkers, R. (2006). "Effectiviteit van subsidies voor giften aan goede doelen". *ESB*, 91(4477): 8-10.

Bekkers, R. (2005). 'Participation in Voluntary Associations: Relations with Resources, Personality, and Political Values'. *Political Psychology*, 26: 439-454.

Bekkers, R. (2004). *Giving and Volunteering in the Netherlands: Sociological and Psychological Perspectives*. (Dissertation Utrecht University).

Bekkers, R. (2003). "Trust, Accreditation, and Philanthropy in the Netherlands". *Nonprofit & Voluntary Sector Quarterly*, 32, 596-615.

Gilder, Dick de, T.N.M. Schuyt, and Melissa Breedijk. 2005. Effects of an Employee Volunteering Program on the Work Force: The ABN-AMRO Case. *Journal of Business Ethics* 61:143-152.

GINS95-07. (1995-2009). Dataset: Giving in the Netherlands Study 1995-2007. VU University Amsterdam.

James III, Russell N. & Pamala Wiepking. (2008). A Comparative Analysis of Educational Donors in the Netherlands. Accepted for publication in the *International Journal of Educational Advancement* 8(2).

Van Lange, P.A.M., Bekkers, R., Schuyt, T.N.M. & Van Vugt, M. (2007). 'From Games to Giving: Social Value Orientation Predicts Donations to Noble Causes'. *Basic & Applied Social Psychology*, 29(4): 375-384.

Leene, G.J.F., and T.N.M. Schuyt. (2008). The Power of the Stranger. Structures and Dynamics of Social Interventions: a Theoretical Framework. Aldershot: Ashgate Publishers.

Meijer, May-May & T.N.M. Schuyt. (2005). Corporate Social Performance as a Bottom Line for Consumers. *Business and Society* 44 (4):442-461.

Wiepking, Pamala & Ineke Maas. forthcoming. Resources That Make You Generous: Effects of Human, Financial, and Social Resources on Charitable Giving. Accepted for publication in Social Forces.

Wiepking, Pamala. 2008. For the Love of Mankind. A Sociological Study on Charitable Giving. (Dissertation VU University Amsterdam).

Wiepking, Pamala. 2007. The Philanthropic Poor: In Search of Explanations for the Relative Generosity of Lower Income Households. Voluntas 18(4): 339-358.

2.10 Spain
Marta Rey García[36]

A methodological approach
When approaching the measurement of household charitable giving in Spain, not only survey design and statistical exploitation methodologies, but also the definition of basic concepts, vary widely. The three key differential points refer to the definitions utilized for "household", "donations" and "charitable organizations" when researching charitable giving.

What do we mean by "household" giving? Private giving to public good causes or philanthropy can be originated from different "donor" categories (Salamon and Anheier 1999). A proposal for a classification that builds on that donor-oriented typology, integrates donation mechanisms, and adapts to Spanish contemporary reality follows:

- Direct household giving during the life of individuals, both to third-party individuals and nonprofits, or by endowing a foundation.
- Direct household giving by will (bequests), both to third-party individuals and nonprofits, or by endowing a foundation.
- Indirect household giving through tax benefits regulated in the Spanish "Nonprofit Organizations and Charitable Giving Fiscal Law" (*Ley 49/2002 de régimen fiscal de las entidades sin fines lucrativos y de los incentivos fiscales al mecenazgo*), i.e. tax credit on the "Tax on Individual Income" (*Impuesto sobre la Renta de las Personas Físicas* or *IRPF*).
- Indirect household giving through differential subsidization mechanisms such as the tax designation scheme implemented in the 0.7% of the "Tax on Individual Income" (López Tello 2008, Carmichael 2008) .[37]

---

[36] Marta Rey García, Facultad de Ciencias Económicas y Empresariales, Universidade da Coruña, Campus de Elviña, A Coruña, Spain, martarey@udc.es, +34 981 167000

[37] "In many jurisdictions, governments subsidize private financial contributions to civic activities that are identified as charitable or publicly-beneficial. The subsidies reduce the price to the donor of transferring a certain quantity of funds to an eligible donee, either by providing the donor with a rebate, a deduction from taxable income, or a credit on taxes otherwise payable, or by providing the donee with a matching grant. Typically, governments that subsidize contributions do at uniform rates. In recent decades, however, several governments have introduced differential subsidies, whereby the subsidy rates differ according to characteristics of either the contributions (their timing and form, and the donee organizations), or the services financed at least in part by those contributions (their recipients, their type)", Carmichael 2008.

- Indirect household giving through official lotteries and private raffles (e.g. *ONCE*, *Asociación Española contra el Cáncer*) and collections (*Cáritas* and NGOs tied to the Catholic Church).
- Corporate giving ("corporate social responsibility", "mecenazgo empresarial", "gasto empresarial en fines de interés general", etc) which includes:
  - direct corporate expenditure.
  - giving through corporate foundations.
  - giving through tax benefits regulated in the 49/2002 Law (tax credit on the "Corporate Tax" or *Impuesto de Sociedades*) and differential subsidization mechanisms (i.e. giving to eligible public good institutions or initiatives prioritized in each year's "State General Budget Law" (*Ley de Presupuestos Generales del Estado*).
  - giving through lotteries and collections.
- A distinctive Spanish feature is the heavy weight of savings banks expenditure on public good initiatives or "obra social". Although Spanish savings banks are themselves financial entities of foundational nature, their "obra social" is nowadays also marketed to stakeholders as corporate social responsibility.
- Nonprofit institutions (foundations, associations, etc) giving, both direct and through tax benefits (tax exemptions on the "Corporate Tax").
- Other institutional giving.

Table 2.10.1 A proposal for a classification of private giving in Spain

Private Giving			
Household Giving		Corporate and Institutional Giving	
Direct	Indirect	Direct	Indirect
• During life of donors • Bequests	• Tax benefits (tax credits) • Differential subsidization mechanisms • Lotteries, raffles and collections	• Corporate expenditures in public good initiatives • Corporate foundations • Independent foundations • Other nonprofits	• Tax benefits (tax credits, tax exemptions) • Differential subsidization mechanisms • Lotteries, raffles and collections

Direct private giving (as opposed to private giving through tax benefits, differential subsidization or lottery mechanisms) can utilize different distribution channels:

- It can be directly donated to the target population by individuals ("man-to-man philanthropy"), corporations or institutions.
- It can be directed to the charitable organizations which donate the aid or deliver the service to the target population.
- It can be donated to intermediary charitable organizations which then refund those nonprofit organizations supplying the aid or service to the target population.

What do we mean by "donations"? The second distinction to be made is between donation of cash or products, i.e. goods or services, which can be easily market-valued, and the donation of time (volunteering). Cash donations are more easily and frequently quantified than in-kind donations; but valuing volunteering is even more difficult. Membership fees or "cuotas" should not be considered donations.

What do we mean by "charitable organizations" in Spain? An important methodological distinction should be made between the fiscal law approach, the nonprofit sector approach and the social economy approach when researching the Third Sector in Spain. The first approach utilizes a narrow definition of "charitable organizations" as stated in the "Nonprofit Organizations and Charitable Giving Fiscal Law" (*Ley 49/2002*), which would include the following:

- foundations (it should be noted that the right to found is recognized in the 1978 Spanish Constitution and therefore enjoys maximum legal protection).
- nonprofit associations only if recognized as such by the Government (*asociaciones declaradas de utilidad pública*). In 2002 only 1,135 out of a total of 268,826 associations had been declared "de utilidad pública" (Ruiz Olabuénaga 2006).
- NGOs for Development.
- Sports federations.
- Federations and Associations of nonprofits.
- Special entities (*entidades singulares*) i.e. the Spanish National Blind Organization (*Organización Nacional de Ciegos* or ONCE), the Spanish Red Cross (*Cruz Roja Española*) and *Cáritas* (Catholic Church-tied).

The nonprofit sector approach, utilized by Lester Salamon's pioneer Johns Hopkins Comparative Nonprofit Sector Project (Salamon and Anheier 1998, 1999; Ruiz Olabuénaga 2000), refers to organized, private, self-governing, non-profit-distributing and voluntary organizations. It excludes religious institutions, and most cooperatives and mutuals. In practice, it includes all foundations and associations, the three special entities mentioned above, a select minority of cooperatives and mutuals, educational centres, sports clubs, hospitals and savings banks with their "obra social".

The social economy approach, originated by the CIRIEC, has been utilized by the ambitious study on *La Economía Social en España,* directed by Professor García Delgado between 2001 and 2004 with the support of Fundación ONCE. This approach extends to all types of nonprofit organizations serving households, plus certain additional categories:

- all cooperatives, mutuals and associations.
- foundations, although only recently.
- the three special entities (*ONCE, Cruz Roja, Cáritas*)
- savings banks as a whole, including their "obra social".
- "sociedades laborales", special employment centers, and insertion firms or "empresas de inserción" created to employ disabled people.

Were this extended approach taken to the limit, even trade unions, political parties, professional and managerial organizations such as the "colegios profesionales", and religious institutions could be considered to some extent to be part of the Third Sector.

Data sources and descriptive statistics for household donations in Spain

Secondary sources: estimating the Third Sector and philanthropic giving in Spain

The first economic estimate of the Third Sector and philanthropic giving in Spain was made by a team directed by Prof. Ruiz Olabuénaga under the international umbrella of Lester Salamon's Johns Hopkins Comparative Nonprofit Sector Project (Salamon and Anheier 1998, 1999; Ruiz Olabuénaga 2000); therefore using the nonprofit approach. The principal data sources used were from the National Statistics Institute of Spain (*Instituto Nacional de Estadística* or *INE*), in charge of the state statistical services, in addition to data available from various government ministries and sociological surveys, both population- and organization-based. According to this study, the expenditures of the nonprofit sector in Spain in 1995 were equivalent to 4.61% of Spain's gross domestic product; 5.87% if volunteer inputs were included. The Spanish nonprofit sector was therefore comparable to that of France, Germany or Austria. Nonprofits revenue came predominantly from fees and charges. Philanthropy came second on the revenue structure and contributed 18.8% of total revenues or, if volunteers inputs were included, up to 36.3%. Household giving, however, was not detailed from other sources (foundations, firms) of philanthropic giving.

This study was partially updated years later (Ruiz Olabuénaga 2006), showing that the expenditures of the nonprofit sector in Spain had grown to 4.7% of Spain's gross domestic product in 2002; 6.4% if volunteering were input. A total of 7,300,000 individuals donated money to nonprofits in 2002, and the weight of philanthropy on their income structure was as follows (once again no details for household giving):

Table 2.10.2 Weight of private giving in the income structure of Spanish associations and foundations (2002)

	Revenues < €100,000 / year	Revenues > €100,000 / year
Associations	12.35%	32.16%
Foundations	33.43%	38.50%

Eighty-one percent of associations and 34% of foundations had total revenues under €100,000 per year. One decade later, the research team directed by Dr. Salamon is trying to secure the implementation of the UN Handbook on Nonprofit Institutions in the National Accounting System of Spain, starting with the creation of a satellite account for the nonprofit sector.

The second economic estimate of the Third Sector and philanthropic giving in Spain was made by a team led by Prof. García Delgado utilizing a social economy approach (García Delgado 2004; Jiménez 2005). This study updated the weight of the Third Sector, including volunteering, to 5.6% of total gross operating surplus (*excedente bruto de explotación*) in 2001; 8.2% if savings banks were taken into account. Utilizing the *Encuesta a Directivos de las entidades, FONCE-2001* as source, philanthropy was quantified at 9.7% of total income of associations and foundations.

A pioneering monographic study about philanthropy in Spain has been undertaken by a team lead by Prof. Pérez Díaz (Pérez Díaz ed. 2008). This study includes a quantitative analysis of private giving in Spain (Sánchez Pérez 2008) with data from the Tax Agency (*Agencia Tributaria*) and the Center for Sociological Research (*Centro de Investigaciones Sociológicas* or *CIS*); and a specific analysis for high-income individuals based on a 2007 monographic survey (Chuliá y Muñoz Comet 2008). This latter survey explores ideas and perceptions about philanthropy among members of boards of directors of listed companies. With a 7% response rate, the survey includes some interesting results:

• 94% of respondents believe philanthropy is little or scarcely developed in Spain and 66% believe it is underdeveloped relative to comparable countries in Europe.

- 56% of respondents believe big philanthropic donations benefit few or very few people.
- 82% think those beneficiaries lack adequate knowledge about donors.
- 89% think neither public opinion/society in general nor politicians value philanthropic activities adequately.
- 80% believe a change in the tax incentives would translate into a significant increase in philanthropic donations.
- 90% agree it is important to educate children in the value of philanthropy.
- 79% participate in the board of a foundation or philanthropic organization, but 47% do not regularly dedicate time to philanthropic activities.

Primary sources: surveys, available statistics and annual reports

The Center for Sociological Research (*Centro de Investigaciones Sociológicas* or *CIS*) is an entity under the umbrella of the Ministry of the Presidency which was established to study Spanish society, mainly through public opinion polls. The *CIS* does not conduct any specific survey on household charitable giving. Some of its past "Barometers" (e.g. 2000, 2001) and publications have touched on citizens and social participation through all types of associations and political parties (Montero et al. 2006), on the connection between NGOs for Development, politics and the media (Jerez et al. 2008), on the public image of the Third Sector and attitudes and behaviours regarding volunteering (De la Torre Prados 2005), or on partial aspects of the associative movement (Ayuso 2007). Neither systematic nor monographic surveys touching on the attitudes and behaviours of individuals regarding philanthropy and nonprofits have been performed by the *CIS*.

The 2006 *CIS* study on citizens and social participation, however, contains interesting data on household donations relative to the self-declared socio-economic status of donors (not to their income level) and to some other socio-demographics (Sánchez Pérez 2008). 51.9% of "technical and intermediate positions" declare to have either donated or fundraised for public good causes during the last twelve months, followed by "office and services workers" (33.3%), "managers and professionals" (32.8%), "small entrepreneurs" (30.7%), "students" (24.5%), "qualified blue-collar workers" (24.4%), and "non-qualified blue-collar workers" (23.9%), among other categories. "Farmers" would be the socio-economic group with the smallest propensity to give/fundraise (only 14%). Those pertaining to upper and medium classes would show a higher propensity to give/fundraise (over 30%

on average), compared to workers (around or below 20%). According to the same study, more than 35% of individuals between 35 and 44 years old and more than 30% of individuals between 45 and 54 years old would have either donated or fundraised, while percentages for younger and elderly people would be around or below 25%.

The Spanish Tax Agency (*Agencia Tributaria*) provides the most valuable and updated data about household giving among those available. Sánchez Pérez (2008) analyses them for the 2005 fiscal year campaign of the "Tax on Individual Income", concluding that private giving in Spain if not an exclusive territory of wealthy individuals:

- 1,794,516 taxpayers (10.5% over total) declared to have donated.
- Declared donations totalled €330,000,000, i.e. an average of €184 per donor.
- Both the percentage of taxpayers declaring donations and the amount donated were directly proportional to income. This relationship between income and amount donated, however, did not hold for taxpayers declaring annual income below €1,500.
- In absolute terms, taxpayers declaring the highest annual income were the most generous, both regarding donors percentage over total and average donations. In relative terms, however, their donations amounted to 0.29% of their income, while the medium-income segments were the most generous with donations amounting to 0.44% of their income.

The National Statistics Institute or *INE* has been producing the Household Budget Continuous Survey (*Encuesta Continua de Presupuestos Familiares*) since 1985, and this provides quarterly and annual information on the origin and amount of household incomes, and the way they are used in several consumption expenditures. Its questionnaires request information about goods and services purchased for final consumption, self-consumption, self-supply, wage in kind and free and semi-free consumption; however, they do not include any questions about household charitable giving since 1992.

The amount of household giving indirectly raised under the 0.7% of the Tax on Individual Income ruling (0.52 % until fiscal year 2006) is published every year. This differential subsidization mechanism allows individuals to voluntarily devote 0.7% of their total tax liability ("cuota íntegra") to charitable purposes. In their tax statement, taxpayers can choose to devote that amount to either the Catholic Church ("Iglesia"), to NGOs active in social action and cooperation ("fines sociales"), to match it and share it among the two with no additional cost (0.7% + 0.7%), or to mark neither of the two options, thus leaving the amount to the State for general purposes. The Ministry of Education, Social Policies and Sports (formerly the Ministry of Work) administers 80% of the funds raised for "fines sociales", distributing them through an annual open contest among social action NGOs; the Ministry of International Affairs does the same with the other 20% among NGOs for Development. The Law of the State General Budgets can put a limit on the amount finally devoted to these calls for subsidies.

According to the *Plataforma de ONG de Acción Social* and for the fiscal year of 2005, 22% of 17,105,088 taxpayers specified Catholic Church only, 33.83% specified "fines sociales" only, 11.36% specified both options, and 32.81% specified none. This means an increase of almost 1 million in the number of taxpayers that specified the "fines socials" option between 2002 and 2005. The figure indirectly raised for NGOs through this tax designation scheme has almost tripled between fiscal year 1999 and fiscal year 2006 (vid. Fig. 2.10.1).

The 0.7% new ruling has been first implemented for fiscal year 2007, resulting in an unprecedented increase from €168,000,000 raised in the previous campaign, to €240,000,000. This increase of over 40% is to be attributed not only to the increase in the percentage over total tax liability (from 0.52% to 0.7%), but also to the publicity campaign carried out by the *Plataforma de ONG de Acción Social* in 2008 to explain this tax designation scheme to taxpayers.

Another primary source to be taken into account consists of annual reports by the most important nonprofits and their coordinating boards. In its 2006

Fig. 2.10.1 Funds raised for NGOs through the 0.52% "Tax on Individual Income" (*IRPF*) differential subsidization mechanism (in euros for a given fiscal year)

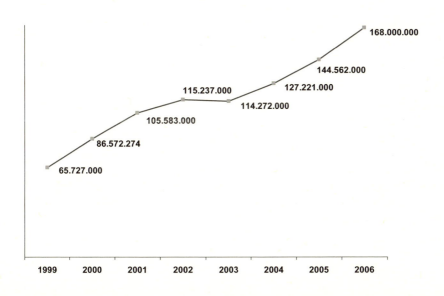

| 1999 | 2000 | 2001 | 2002 | 2003 | 2004 | 2005 | 2006 |

report, the Spanish Coordinator of NGOs for Development (*Coordinadora de Organizaciones no Gubernamentales para el Desarrollo de España* or *CONDGE*) included data relative to private donations received by its over 100 member organizations for international cooperation programs. These organizations include big NGOs such as *Ayuda en Acción*, *UNICEF*, *Intermón Oxfam*, the Catholic *Manos Unidas* or *Médicos del Mundo*, and special entities such as *Cáritas Española* or *Cruz Roja Española*. According to this report, direct household donations amounted to €135,462,305 in 2005, meaning 25% of total income. Household donations increased 47% relative to 2004, this variation being closely connected to emergency campaigns undertaken on the occasion of the South East Asia tsunami. Eight NGOs absorbed more than 90% of the 2005 household donations figure, Manos Unidas being the top beneficiary. By contrast, membership fees and other recurrent quotas paid for by individuals (e.g. for godfathering children) amounted to €90,210,000 in 2005. A total of 20,296 people volunteered their time to these NGOs. Forty-one percent devoted 2-4 hours per week, 36% devoted 4-10 hours per week, and 23% devoted more than 10 hours.

Although some of the most relevant *CONGDE* member organizations are active in other areas, all data in this report refer exclusively to their international development and cooperation projects. If all their activities were taken into account, total income would double and household donation figures would grow accordingly. A good example would be the Spanish Red Cross, whose total income for 2004 amounted to €373,442,285. Total household donations amounted to slightly over 9% of total income, with approximately €23,000,000 being raised through the "Gran Premio del Oro", the National Lottery and other raffles, and €12,000,000 through emergency campaigns. International cooperation, however, amounted only to €39,000,000, equivalent to 11% of its total expenditures for the year. *Cáritas*, the confederation coordinating charitable organizations belonging to the Catholic Church in Spain, is another relevant example. Household donations accounted for 61.7 % of its 2005 total income. With total expenditures of €170,000,000 during that year, €23,000,000 were devoted to international cooperation.

The *Plataforma de ONG de Acción Social* groups 25 member organizations including special entities such as *ONCE*, *Cáritas* and *Cruz Roja Española*, NGOs for Development such as *Medicos del Mundo*, and relevant social action NGOs such as the Spanish Association against Cancer (*Asociación Española contra el Cáncer* or *AECC*), which attract a considerable volume of household donations. As far as we know, the Platform does not publish aggregated economic data about its members, unlike the *CONGDE*, and annual reports of each member organization do not always separate household donations from other philanthropic income. One example would be the *ONCE*, with total income for 2007 amounting to €2,813,102,000, but no details concerning the portion originating from household donations through the different lotteries and gambling managed by this nonprofit corporation. Another example would be the *AECC*, whose total income for 2007, according its annual report, amounted to €47,773,580. Of this amount, €23,598,823 came from household donations, including lotteries, collections, direct donations and bequests.

To conclude, the following strong points of these primary data sources and descriptive statistics could be mentioned:

- The Spanish Tax Agency provides accurate and yearly updated data on direct individual donations as declared under the Tax on Individual Income. These data are aggregated for segments of income. Differential subsidization through the 0.7% of the Individual Income Tax also provides accurate, annually updated, and aggregated data on indirect household giving.
- The majority of household giving concentrates on special entities such as the Spanish Red Cross, *ONCE* or *Cáritas*, or on big NGOs such as *Manos Unidas, AECC, UNICEF, Ayuda en Acción* or *Intermón Oxfam*. These organizations include information on donations received in their annual reports, and sometimes separate data on household giving from other income sources.

Weak points would include:
- There is an urgent need to combine data from the Spanish Tax Agency with socio-demographic data on individual and household donor units, which could be gathered at a little incremental cost through both the National Statistics Institute Household Budget Continuous Survey (*Encuesta Continua de Presupuestos Familiares*), and the Center for Sociological Research "barometers" and other surveys.
- The Spanish National Accounting System does not include any specific account for either social economy or Third Sector organizations, or for household charitable giving. All approaches to aggregate charitable giving based on available statistics are therefore partial and/or indirect estimates (e.g. volunteering, weight of domestic giving over total income of nonprofits), and most sources do not separate private household giving from private corporate and institutional giving.
- Duplicities may occur. A typical example are intra-sector donations, i.e. household donations to intermediary charitable organizations which then refund to other nonprofits. Data on household giving to foundations or to associations may overlap with data on household giving to NGOs for Development, as 44% of these nonprofits choose

the legal formula of association to incorporate and 36% choose the foundation formula. Giving to the Spanish Red Cross international cooperation projects may be accounted for twice if data from its annual statement are added to the *CONGDE* data.

- Neither all-inclusive nor partial household giving surveys are carried out on an annual basis. Both longitudinal and transversal comparisons incorporating socio-demographic data on donors are therefore difficult or even impossible to make.

Conclusion

Spain urgently needs to improve its data gathering and research capacity regarding philanthropy in general and household charitable giving in particular. The notorious growth and strengthening of Spanish civil society since the transition to Democracy, be it measured in terms of social economy or Third Sector activity, or in terms of changing social attitudes and philanthropic giving, demands that household giving be researched and mapped accordingly.

Official surveys and statistics do not pay attention to household giving, thus necessarily limiting its presence in excellent secondary sources such as the comprehensive research projects directed by Ruiz Olabuénaga or García Delgado; the exception being the monographic study carried out by the team lead by Pérez Díaz about private giving. These studies are not repeated periodically, which would undoubtedly require both strong economic and political support, nor do they always separate household giving from corporate and institutional giving, presenting "philanthropic income" or "philanthropic donations" as a whole. Regarding primary sources, the lack of socio-demographic data on donors and/or comparable time series on donor attitudes, profiles and donations reinforces this trend. In relative terms, private corporate and institutional giving, and particularly philanthropy from foundations and listed or big firms, has received much more attention than household giving (Projecció 2003, Fundación Luis Vives 2004).

Support from the *INE* and the *CIS* is essential for advancing both population-based and organization-based economic approaches to household giving, and also for complementing data disclosed by the Spanish Tax Agency on declared individual donations. Furthermore, an organization-based economic approach would require, on the first place, strong coordination among state and autonomous administrations relative to public register data, and also among different nonprofit platforms and networks (Spanish Association of Foundations or *AEF*, *CONGDE*, *Plataforma de ONG de Acción Social*, etc.). Secondly, a clear transparency policy relative to donation data disclosure in annual reports, aligned with the efforts already made in this direction by *CONGDE* members and other relevant Spanish nonprofits, would be also needed.

The lack of visibility of household giving in Spain is mainly a consequence of the relative absence of the Spanish Third Sector in terms of official statistics and surveys. As long as the macro magnitudes of the Third Sector are not gathered in the National Accounting System as a separate, relevant and new sector of the economy; and until the activity of nonprofit organizations is evaluated with adequate criteria which put a value on specificities such as volunteer inputs and positive externalities (i.e. the effect of nonprofit activities on social welfare and integration, educational and cultural development or territorial equilibrium), the Third Sector will remain in a shadow zone and household giving will be underestimated.

References

Agencia Tributaria (AEAT). www.aeat.es

Asociación Española Contra el Cáncer (2008). *Informe anual 2007.* www.todocancer.org

Ayuso Sánchez, L. (2007). *Las asociaciones familiares en España*, CIS, Madrid.

Cabra de Luna, M.A. (1998). *El tercer sector y las fundaciones de España hacia el nuevo milenio. Enfoque económico, sociológico y jurídico*, Escuela Libre Editorial, Madrid.

Carmichael, C. M. (2008). "Doing Good Better? The Differential Subsidization of Charitable Contributions", paper presented to the ISTR Conference, Barcelona.

Centro de Investigaciones Sociológicas (CIS). www.cis.es

Coordinadora de Organizaciones no Gubernamentales para el Desarrollo de España (2007). *Informe de la CONGDE sobre el sector de las ONGD 2006*, Madrid.

Cruz Roja Española, (2005). *Memoria 2004.* www.cruzroja.es

Chuliá, E. & Muñoz Comet, J. (2008), "En torno a la filantropía de las élites económicas en España. Un estudio empírico como punto de partida", in Pérez-Díaz, V. (ed.), *La filantropía: tendencias y perspectivas*, Fundación de Estudios Financieros, Madrid.

De la Torre Prados, I. (2005). *Tercer Sector y participación ciudadana en España*, CIS, Madrid.

Fundación Luis Vives (2004). *Anuario del mecenazgo empresarial de la acción social*, Madrid.

García Delgado, J.L. (Dir.) (2004). *Las cuentas de la economía social: el tercer sector en España*, Thomson Civitas, Madrid.

Instituto Nacional de Estadística (INE). www.ine.es

Jérez, A., Sampedro, V. & López Rey, J.A. (2008). *Del 0,7% a la desobediencia civil. Política e información del movimiento y las ONG de Desarrollo*, CIS, Madrid.

Jiménez, J.C. (coord.) (2005). *Un enfoque económico del Tercer Sector*, Fundación ONCE, Madrid.

Ley 49/2002, de 23 de diciembre, de regimen fiscal de las entidades sin fines lucrativos y de los incentivos fiscales al mecenazgo.

Ley 50/2002, de 26 de diciembre, de Fundaciones.

López Tello, J., "Sobre la filantropía y los impuestos", in Pérez-Díaz, V. (ed.), *La filantropía: tendencias y perspectivas*, Fundación de Estudios Financieros, Madrid.

Marcuello Servós, C. (coord.) (2007). *Capital social y organizaciones no lucrativas en España. El caso de las ONGD*, Fundación BBVA, Madrid.

Ministerio de Economía y Hacienda. www.estadief.meh.es

Ministerio de Trabajo y Asuntos Sociales. (2005). *Quién es quién. Las entidades de acción social beneficiarias de la asignación tributaria del 0,52% del IRPF, convocatoria 2004*, Madrid.

Montero, J.R., Font, J. & Torcal, M. (2006). *Ciudadanos, asociaciones y participación en España*, CIS, Madrid.

ONCE (2008), *Memoria 2007 de la ONCE y su Fundación*. www.once.es

Pérez-Díaz, V. & López Novo, J.P. (2003). *El Tercer Sector Social en España*. Madrid, Ministerio de Trabajo y Asuntos Sociales.

Plataforma de ONG de Acción Social (2008). *La asignación tributaria del IRPF y la Acción Social*, www.plataformaong.org

Projeccio Mecenatge Social. (2003). *Directorio 2002 del Patrocinio, Mecenazgo y Responsabilidad Social Corporativa en España*, Barcelona.

Ruiz Olabuénaga, J.I. (Dir.) (2006). *El sector no lucrativo en España. Una visión reciente*, Fundación BBVA.

Ruiz Olabuénaga, J.I. (Dir.) (2000), *El sector no lucrativo en España*, Fundación BBV, Bilbao.

Salamon, L.M., Anheier, H.K. et al. (1998), *The Emerging Sector Revisited. A Summary*, The Johns Hopkins Center for Civil Society Studies, Baltimore, MD.

Salamon, L.M., Anheier, H.K. et al. (1999), *Global Civil Society: Dimensions of the Nonprofit Sector*, The Johns Hopkins Center for Civil Society Studies, Baltimore, MD.

Sánchez Pérez, E.J. (2008), "Evolución y situación actual de la filantropía en España", in Pérez-Díaz, V. (ed.), *La filantropía: tendencias y perspectivas*, Fundación de Estudios Financieros, Madrid.

Schuyt, Th.N.M., Gouwenberg, B.M., Meijer, M.M., Bekkers, R.H.F.P. & Wiepking, P. (2007). *Geven in Nederland 2007. Giften, Legaten, Sponsoring en Vrijwillligerswerk*, Reed Business, Ámsterdam.

VV.AA. (2001), *La realidad de las Fundaciones en España. Análisis sociológico, psicosocial y económico*, Santander, Fundación Marcelino Botín.

2.11 Sweden
Lars-Erik Olsson[38] and Lars Svedberg[39]

Sweden has a long tertiary sector tradition with strong historical roots, which is currently being challenged by internal events as well as external ones. It is important to note that Sweden's membership of the European Union (EU) is now just over a decade old and tertiary sector is being put under pressure. The Swedish tertiary sector model, which is labelled the "popular mass movement model" and is characterized by a strong, historically rooted tradition of membership-based ownership, democratic structure, and voluntary work, exhibits features that distinguish the sector in Sweden (and other Nordic countries) from that of many other countries of Europe

The voluntary work that people carry out includes a number of tasks, either within the framework of voluntary organisations in the form of volunteering, or in the form of informal help- and care giving to family members, neighbours, friends or colleagues. The scope of these different types of activities in Sweden represents more than half a million full-time jobs on a yearly basis in 2005.

Volunteering
Repeated population surveys over a span of 13 years have been carried out by Ersta Sköndal University College and these indicate that Swedish volunteer work not only continues to be extensive, but it is also quite stable. A little more than 50 percent of the population is regularly engaged in volunteering and the time that people devote to this type of work has even increased a little since the previous survey (performed in 1998). It can be seen as a distinct feature of the popular mass movement model to work as a volunteer. During a period of more than 10 years, three major population studies have been conducted. According to the data, the population performs voluntary work (see Table 2.11.1).

Table 2.11.1 Voluntary work 1992, 1998 and 2005. Percentage of the grown-up population (16-74 years) involved in voluntary work

1992	1998	2005
48	52	51

[38] Lars-Erik Olsson, Ersta Sköndal University College, Insitutionen för Socialt Arbete, Sköndal, Sweden, lars-erik.olsson@esh.se, +46 (0)8-555 051 32
[39] Lars Svedberg, Ersta Sköndal University College, Stockholm, Sweden, Lars.svedberg@esh.se, +46 (0)8-555 051 37

The average volunteer carries out approximately 14 hours voluntary work per month, which is high, also from an international point of view. The common discourse on civic involvement stating that this type of involvement is rapidly declining, and that social capital is eroding, is not supported in our results. However, the more traditional, Scandinavian popular mass movement way of civic engagement may be at risk of being eroded. Our results show signs of this process actually taking place: Membership in voluntary organisations (which is the traditional bridge into volunteering in the Swedish context) has significantly diminished. This is particularly true for women and young people. Volunteering in political parties and other political organisations continues to fall. Other forms of engagement appear, however, as indicated by the results from the survey of 2005. Taking this into account, there is no reason to be singularly negative about the development of civic engagement in Sweden.

The value basis of volunteering is strongly supported by the Swedish people. It is primarily considered as a "force of its own" which should not be confused with paid work or household work. Even if volunteers can be found in all different age groups, socio-economic groups and among ethnic Swedes as well as immigrants, the "typical volunteer" is a man or woman in the midst of their career, well-educated and well-integrated, who has children, is a born Swede, and who originates from a family who has a tradition of civic involvement. Furthermore, the typical volunteer has more informal networks than the average Swede and is more often engaged in regular informal help- or care giving than the average Swede.

It is possible to observe a socio-economic resource pattern among volunteers. Men and women with higher education and income were more likely to be volunteers. Men and women with a lower degree of education and income were less likely to be volunteers. We could also see that volunteering could be a family pattern, learned from one generation to another.

Explanatory factors for volunteer work can be summarised into three patterns. One has to do with the access to social arenas: People who are exposed to one type of arena are more likely to access other arenas as well. Hence, people involved in paid work, who are parents, etc., are more likely to volunteer than others. Another explanatory pattern has to do with access to socio-economic resources, a third has to do with civic traditions. Volunteering is not "instead of" other activities. Rather, there is a pattern of "in addition to" in the results: Both paid work and volunteering, both other civic involvement and volunteering, etc. The same pattern has been found in other countries. There are grounds for speaking about a cumulative social citizenship. Conversely, volunteering does not seem to function as a bridge into society for marginalized people. In a certain sense, a pattern of polarisation can be distinguished in the results, where a rather large group finds itself outside the civic arena.

Voluntary work in Sweden follows to some extent the contour and organisational structure of the welfare state. But the state has in some sense "crowded out" voluntary work in the field of welfare (compared to other European countries) and the voluntary work now being done is mainly in the area of leisure, sports and culture. But bearing that in mind, the welfare-related tertiary sector is still significant when it comes to voluntary work, especially among women.

Sweden has experienced a low degree of professionalization within the tertiary sector compared to other European countries. But we have seen a recent development – between 1992 and 2002 – where the figures show an increase of nearly 9 percent employed in the sector (from 121,000 to nearly 132,000).

Table 2.11.2 Number of employees in the welfare domain

	Public sector	Private sector	Tertiary sector	Total
Number of employees 1990	+/- 840,000	+/- 6,000	+/- 32,000	+/- 900,000
Number of employees 2000	+/- 780,000	+/- 72,000	+/- 29,000	+/- 880,000

In 2005, the total amount of employees was 1 million in the welfare domain, 85 percent of whom were employed in the public sector and around 5 percent in the tertiary sector. The private sector has grown fast in the last decade.

We know that around 130,000 are employed in the tertiary sector, some 35,000 of whom are employed in the welfare domain.

We can also estimate the time that the volunteers in the tertiary sector in total are giving to be around 400,000 FTEs, and that can be compared with the employed to be circa 130,000 FTE in the whole tertiary sector. The characteristic of the Swedish tertiary sector is still one of volunteering, even though the level of memberships is decreasing and becoming more European.

Giving time to relatives and next of kin
While the extent of volunteering has remained stable since it was previously mapped, the extent of informal help- and care giving has increased considerably. In 2005, about 50 percent of the Swedish people were engaged in regular help- and care giving to family members or other close relations. Twenty-two percent of those help people who have particular care needs, i.e. disabled, ill or frail old people, while 28 percent help one or more persons without such specific care needs. The increase in informal helping and caring that can be observed must be assumed to concern help to both types of recipients. Informal help- and care giving is a heterogeneous phenomenon, and the pattern of increase that can be observed may be interpreted in divergent ways: As an expression of a vital Swedish civil society with a great helping potential, or as a response to decreasing care resources from the public sector to those in need. This latter interpretation would be a validation of the pattern of informalisation of public welfare services, which have been noted by other researchers in recent years.

Giving money
In the population study of 2005, we asked volunteers how much money they had donated in the previous 12 months. Unfortunately we could not use these answers due to the Tsunami catastrophe that occurred during these 12 months and this affected people's willingness to give money profoundly.

With the population study of 2005, we have captured patterns of social capital at both the individual level and the societal level. This study confirms the picture of Sweden as a country of strong social capital, on the one hand. On the other hand, Sweden seems to be in the midst of a significant transformation process with is corresponding complications – at least regarding the long-standing Scandinavian tradition of civic engagement.

References

Olsson, L-E., Nordfeldt, M., Larsson, O. and Kendall, J. (2009), 'Sweden: When strong third sector historical roots meet EU policy processes' in J. Kendall (ed.), *Handbook on Third Sector Policy in Europe: Multi Level Processes and Organised Civil Society*, Edward Elgar.

Olsson L-E., Svedberg, L. & Jeppsson Grassman, E., (2005). *Medborgarnas insatser och engagemang i civilsamhället.* Regeringskansliet, Justitiedepartementet.

SCB (2004). 2004:18, Skola, vård och omsorg i privat regi. En sammanställning av statistik. SCB: Örebro.

Svedberg, L. & Lundström, T. (2003). The Voluntary Sector in a Social Democratic Welfare State – The Case of Sweden. In *Journal of Social Policy*, 32,(2), 217-238.

2.12 United Kingdom
Cathy Pharoah[40]

There are several main sources of data on individual and household giving in the UK. The situation is somewhat similar to the US, where there are several good surveys but with striking variations in their results, because giving survey results are highly sensitive to any differences in the methodologies used.

Data sources

Annual
Individual Giving survey series (1987- present)
A longstanding annual sample population survey of <u>individual</u> giving, funded by voluntary organisations. It is currently carried out through a module of questions placed in the Office of National Statistics Omnibus Survey, three times per year. It uses a random probability sample of private households, interviewing one adult per household about personal giving. Sample of +/- 5,000 per year.

Expenditure and Food Survey
The Government's annual sample population survey of <u>household</u> expenditure contains a suite of questions on household giving to charity, including regular deductions from salary which cover charitable giving commitments. The survey has an annual sample of around 7,000 and has been running for 30 years. It excludes charitable purchases from its definition of 'giving'.

Bi-annual
Citizenship Survey
The Government's Citizenship survey covers a range of activities, including individual memberships, volunteering, and some questions on giving. The sample is 10,000 with an ethnic minority booster sample.

Government administrative data
HM Revenue and Customs publishes annual data on the cost of personal charitable tax reliefs on all the various tax-effective ways of giving, including legacies. HMRC is looking at the possibility of allowing individual tax records to be used for research within controlled circumstances.

---

[40] Cathy Pharoah, Co-Director, ESRC Research Centre for Charitable Giving and Philanthropy, Cass Business School, London, United Kingdom, Catherina.Pharoah.1@city.ac.uk, +44 20 7040 8600

One-off national surveys
'Helping Out' was a very good large national sample survey of individual giving and volunteering, with an ethnic minority booster sample.

'Populist' surveys
The annual 'Generosity Index' of wealthy givers, published by the Sunday Times in its Rich List supplement, asks the 1,000 wealthiest people in the UK about their giving.

British Market Research Board Consumer Surveys
Small number of annual questions about individual giving in very large consumer surveys.

Review

Table 2.12.1 Strengths and weaknesses of UK data

Strengths	Weaknesses
Individual Giving survey series	
• Long-term	• Discontinuities in the annual data arise from changes in its funding, ownership and methodology over the years *(initially commissioned by the Charities Aid Foundation (CAF) in 1987, then by NCVO from 1995-2001, and jointly between NCVO/CAF from 2002 onwards)*
• Broadly continuous	
• Well-developed questions	
• Comprehensive coverage of amounts given, use of tax-effective and other methods of giving, and causes supported	
• Good set of background demographic and socio-economic data	• Sample size and frequency are not sufficient for accurate monitoring of seasonal trends or measuring major giving
• Data is publicly available two years after publication	
	• Continuation of survey depends on annual commitment of funding by charities
Expenditure and Food Survey	
• Large, government-funded survey	• Not easy to analyse
• Longitudinal	• Excludes all charitable purchasing
• Fairly continuous	• Does not cover causes
• Excellent set of background demographic and socio-economic data	• Limited coverage of methods of giving

Strengths	Weaknesses
• Scope to link giving expenditure to other household expenditure • Opportunity to track regular monthly charitable payments • Collects giving data through detailed two-week diaries of spending • Data is publicly available	

Citizenship Survey

• Large, government-funded survey • Scope to link giving behaviour to other forms of citizenship • Ethnic minority booster samples • Longitudinal • Data is publicly available	• Limited range of questions on giving

Government administrative data

• Longitudinal • Complete for tax-payers • Data is publicly available	• Only covers tax-effective giving • Only provides aggregate figures by method of giving, and is not broken down by, for example, income band

Note: Data from the 'Helping Out' survey is also publicly available, but not data from private surveys such as the BMRB, or the Sunday Times.

Descriptive statistics

Participation and amounts
The Individual Giving Survey currently estimates UK Giving at about £9.5 billion, and around 1% of average income.

However, results from different individual giving surveys vary considerably. For example:

How much people give - average monthly giving is most recently estimated at:

£26.53   *(NCVO/CAF UK Giving 2007)*
£31.00   *(Helping Out, Office of the Third Sector, 2007)*

How many people give – the monthly proportion who give is estimated at:

54% *(NCVO/CAF UK Giving 2007)*
81% *(Helping Out, OTS, 2007).*

Estimates from the Expenditure and Food Survey tend to come out at about half of this amount, because of the exclusion of charitable purchasing. Analysis of the long-term trend data in this survey has shown a slow decline over the last 30 years in the proportion of households giving to charity, while average household giving has gone up.

Tax-effective giving

Around one-third of the amount given in the UK is estimated to be tax-effective, and around one-third of donors are estimated to use tax-effective giving methods. Tax repaid to charities on giving through Gift Aid - the most popular tax-effective method in the UK which accounts for 90% of all giving - is worth around £850 million: tax repaid to donors is around £200 million.

Causes supported

The NCVO/CAF Individual Giving Survey estimates current support for causes as:

Table 2.12.2 Share of total individual giving by cause, 2006/07

Cause	Share of total giving (%)
Medical research	17
Religious	16
Children/ young people	12
Hospital/ hospices	11
Overseas	9
Education	6
Animal rescue	5
Disability	4
Homelessness	3
Environment	3

Cause	Share of total giving (%)
Sports	3
Elderly	2
Health	2
Arts	<1
Other	7

References

CAF. 2006a. "International Comparisions of Charitable Giving." CAF, London, United Kingdom.

CAF. 2006b. "UK Giving 2005/06. Results of the 2005/06 Survey of Individual Charitable Giving in the UK." CAF, London, United Kingdom.

CAF. 2007. "UK Giving 2006/07. Results of the 2006/07 Individual Giving Survey." CAF, London, United Kingdom.

CAF/NCVO. 2005. UK Giving 2004/2005. London, United Kingdom: CAF/NCVO.

Low, Natalie, Sarah Butt, Angela Ellis Paine, and Justin Davis Smith. 2007. "Helping Out: A National Survey of Volunteering and Charitable Giving." National Center for Social Research / Institute for Volunteering Research, London, United Kingdom.

3. Conclusion
Pamala Wiepking[41]

In this publication, members of the European Research Network on Philanthropy give an overview of the state of philanthropic research in Europe. The result provides much-anticipated insights into the study of philanthropy in twelve European countries. Summarizing these contributions, what conclusions can we draw concerning the current state of philanthropic research in Europe?

We can conclude that research on philanthropy in Europe is being conducted in a variety of ways. The results of this publication show that individual researchers and institutions in different countries are seriously studying philanthropy. For most countries, both population surveys and aggregated data on giving are available. However, the majority of surveys have been conducted in an ad hoc manner and lack consistency over time and between countries, making it difficult to draw useful comparisons. The chapters on the different countries give detailed insights into the exact information available.

For the future of philanthropic research, it is of utmost importance that researchers start collaborating with each other. The European Research Network on Philanthropy can facilitate such collaborations. By working together, we will be able to study philanthropy in Europe from a similar viewpoint, and with comparable methodologies. This will help us gain more insight into the fascinating phenomenon of philanthropy. Working in a research network will also facilitate the study of philanthropy from a comparative perspective.

This collaboration is necessary if we want to answer essential questions on the subject of philanthropy. Examples of important questions that can be answered through international collaborative research include: Why are people in some countries more generous than people in other countries? What effects do governmental subsidies for charitable organizations have on private donations to these organizations? What are the effects of different tax regimes on the incidence and level of charitable donations?

This first publication of the European Research Network on Philanthropy shows that there is a bright future for the study of philanthropy in Europe. By joining forces, we can help to answer these key questions, thereby advancing the field of philanthropic studies.

---

[41] Pamala Wiepking, Department of Philanthropic Studies, VU University Amsterdam, Amsterdam, the Netherlands, P.Wiepking@fsw.vu.nl, +31 (0)20 598 69 22